FOR ORGANS, PIANOS & ELECTRONIC KEYBOARDS

E-Z PLAY® TODAY

219

CHRISTMAS SONGS
WITH 3 CHORDS

ISBN 978-0-634-03291-2

HAL•LEONARD®
CORPORATION

7777 W. BLUEMOUND RD. P.O. BOX 13819 MILWAUKEE, WI 53213

Visit Hal Leonard Online at
www.halleonard.com

Angels We Have Heard on High

Registration 3
Rhythm: Classical or March

Traditional French Carol
Translated by James Chadwick

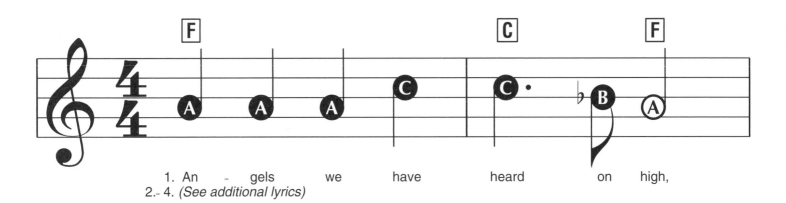

1. An - gels we have heard on high,
2.- 4. *(See additional lyrics)*

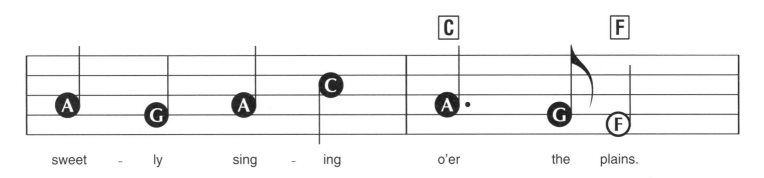

sweet - ly sing - ing o'er the plains.

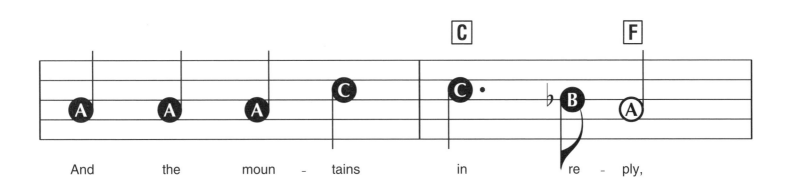

And the moun - tains in re - ply,

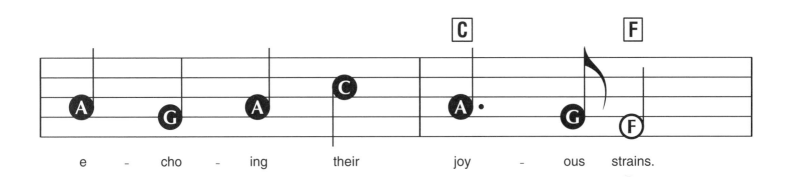

e - cho - ing their joy - ous strains.

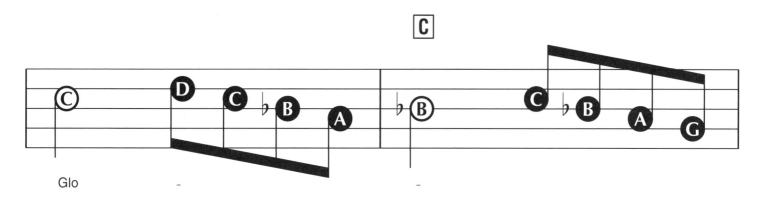

Glo - -

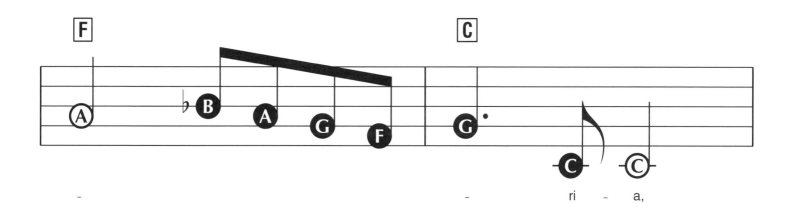

- - ri - a,

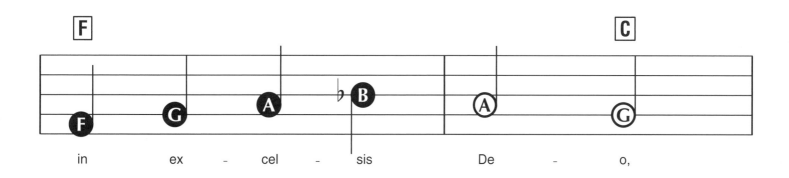

in ex - cel - sis De - o,

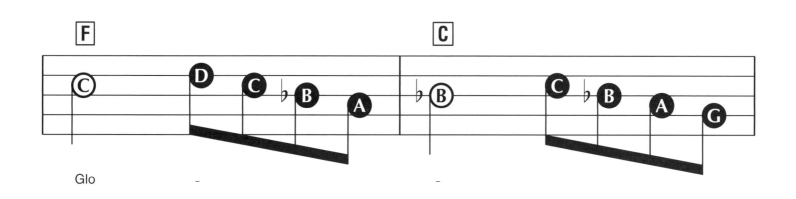

Glo - -

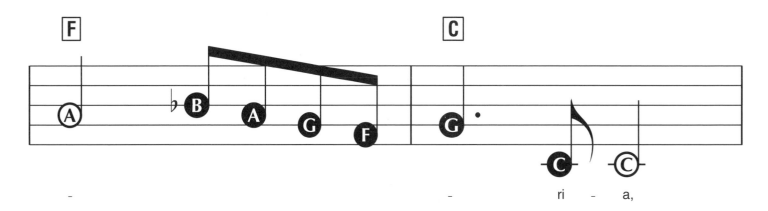

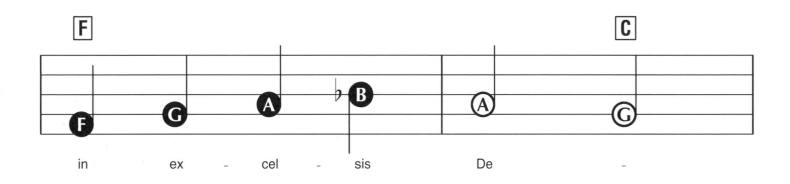

in   ex – cel – sis   De   –

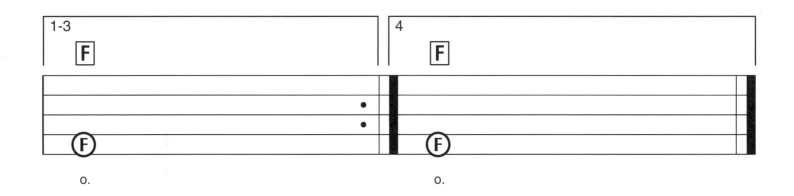

o.   o.

Additional Lyrics

2. Shepherds, why this jubilee?
   Why your joyous strains prolong?
   Say what may the tidings be,
   Which inspire your heavenly song?

   Gloria, in excelsis Deo,
   Gloria, in excelsis Deo.

3. Come to Bethlehem and see,
   Him whose birth the angels sing.
   Come, adore on bended knee,
   Christ the Lord, the newborn King!

   Gloria, in excelsis Deo,
   Gloria, in excelsis Deo.

4. See within a manger laid
   Jesus, Lord of heaven and earth!
   Mary, Joseph, lend your aid,
   With us sing our Savior's birth.

   Gloria, in excelsis Deo,
   Gloria, in excelsis Deo.

Deck the Hall

Registration 5
Rhythm: Classical or Baroque

Traditional Welsh Carol

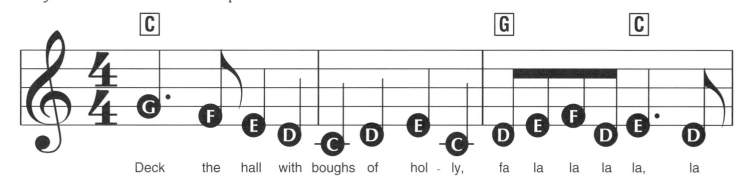

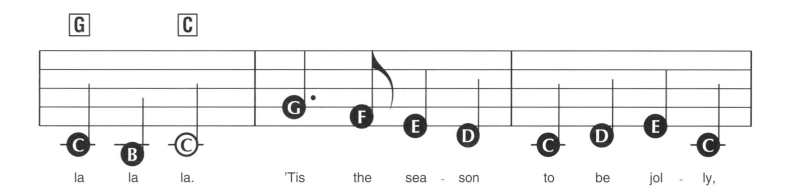

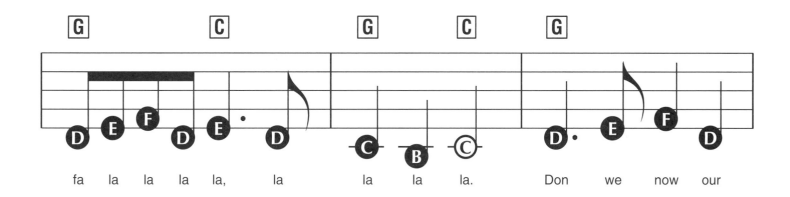

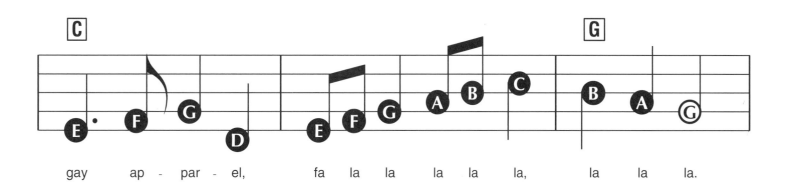

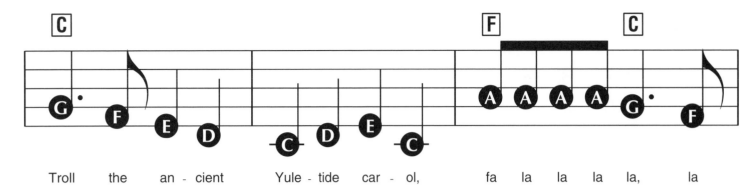

Troll the an-cient Yule-tide car-ol, fa la la la la, la

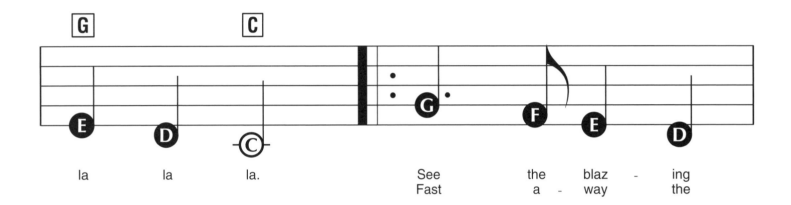

la la la. See the blaz-ing
Fast a - way the

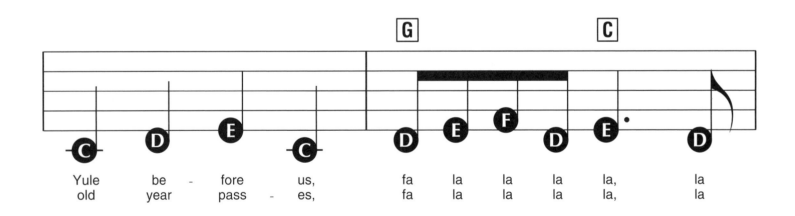

Yule be-fore us, fa la la la la, la
old year pass-es, fa la la la la, la

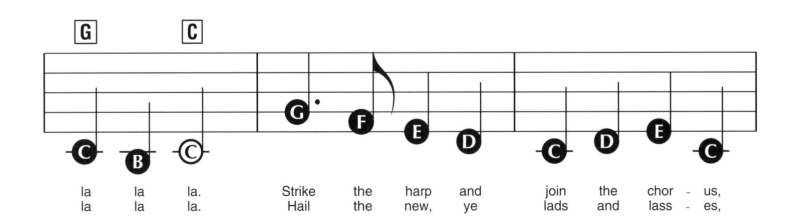

la la la. Strike the harp and join the chor-us,
la la la. Hail the new, ye lads and lass-es,

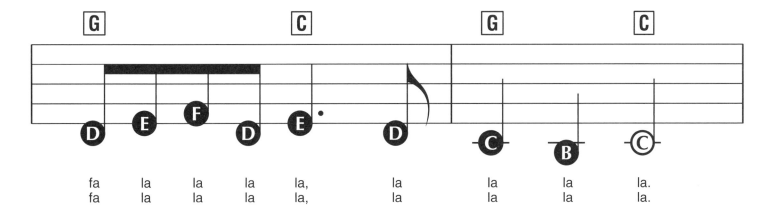

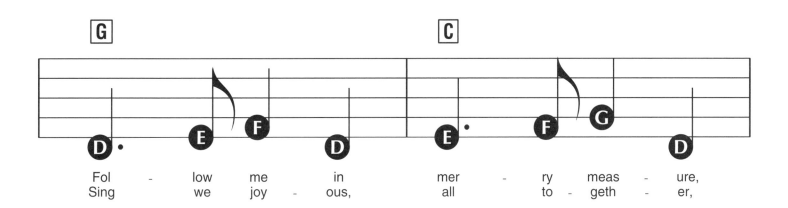

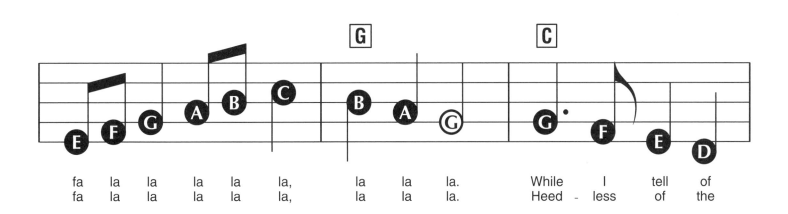

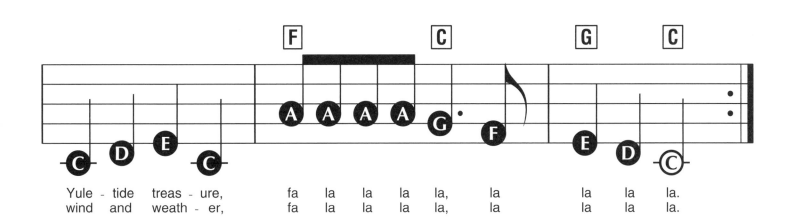

Away in a Manger

Registration 4
Rhythm: Waltz

Anonymous Text (vv.1,2)
Text by John T. McFarland (v.3)
Music by Jonathan E. Spillman

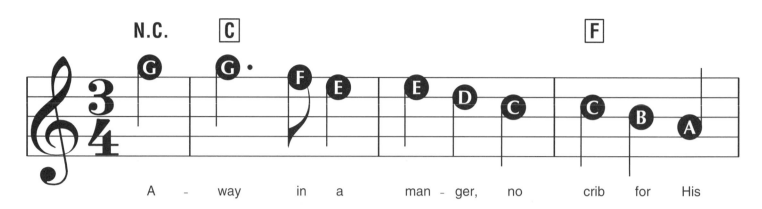

A - way in a man - ger, no crib for His

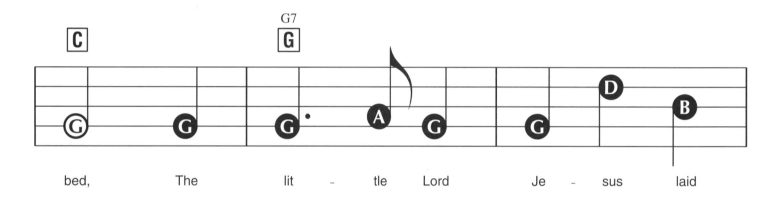

bed, The lit - tle Lord Je - sus laid

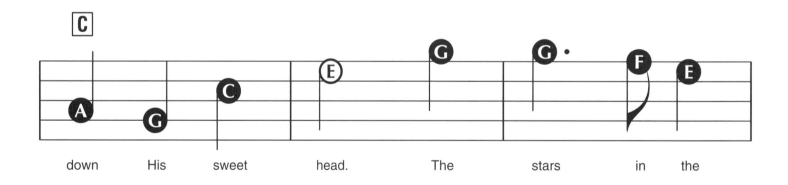

down His sweet head. The stars in the

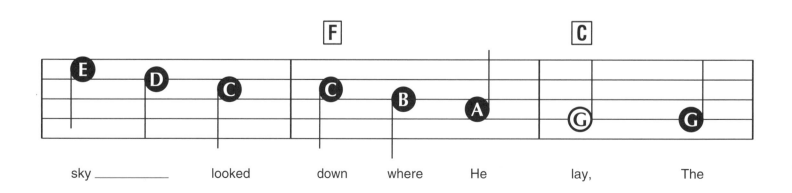

sky _____ looked down where He lay, The

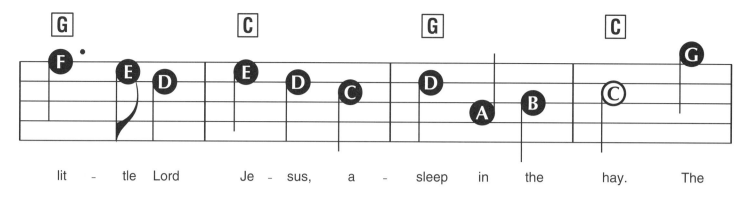

lit - tle Lord   Je - sus,   a -   sleep in the   hay.   The

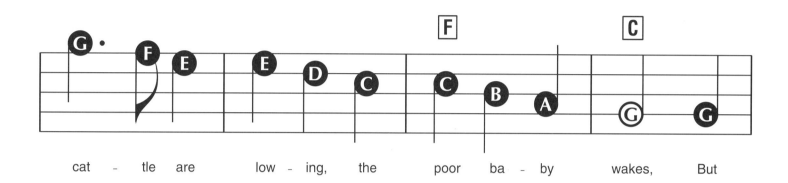

cat - tle are   low - ing,   the   poor ba - by   wakes,   But

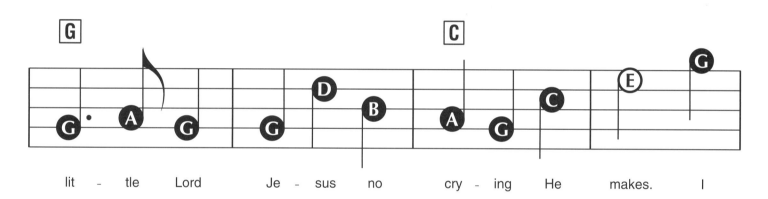

lit - tle Lord   Je - sus   no   cry - ing He   makes.   I

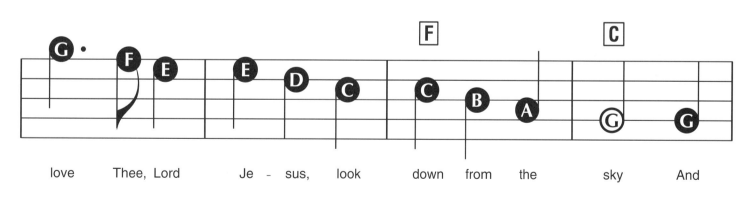

love   Thee, Lord   Je - sus,   look   down from the   sky   And

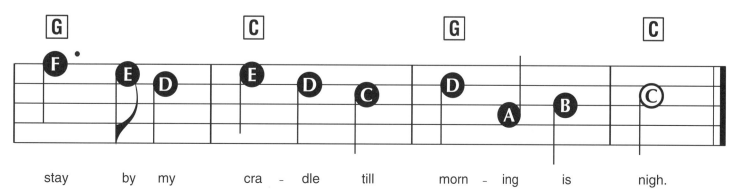

stay   by   my   cra - dle   till   morn - ing is   nigh.

Bring a Torch, Jeannette, Isabella

Registration 3
Rhythm: Waltz

17th Century French Provençal Carol

G   D

D G G ♯F G A B C

Bring   a   torch, _____ Jean - nette, Is - a -
Has - ten   now, _____ good   folk   of   the

G

B A D G G ♯F G

bel - la,   Bring   a   torch, _____ come
vil - lage,   Has - ten   now, _____ the

D   G

A B A G• D D

swift - ly   and   run.   Christ   is
Christ Child   to   see.   You   will

D C B B A G G ♯F

born,   tell   the   folk   of   the   vil - lage,
find   Him   a - sleep   in   a   man - ger,

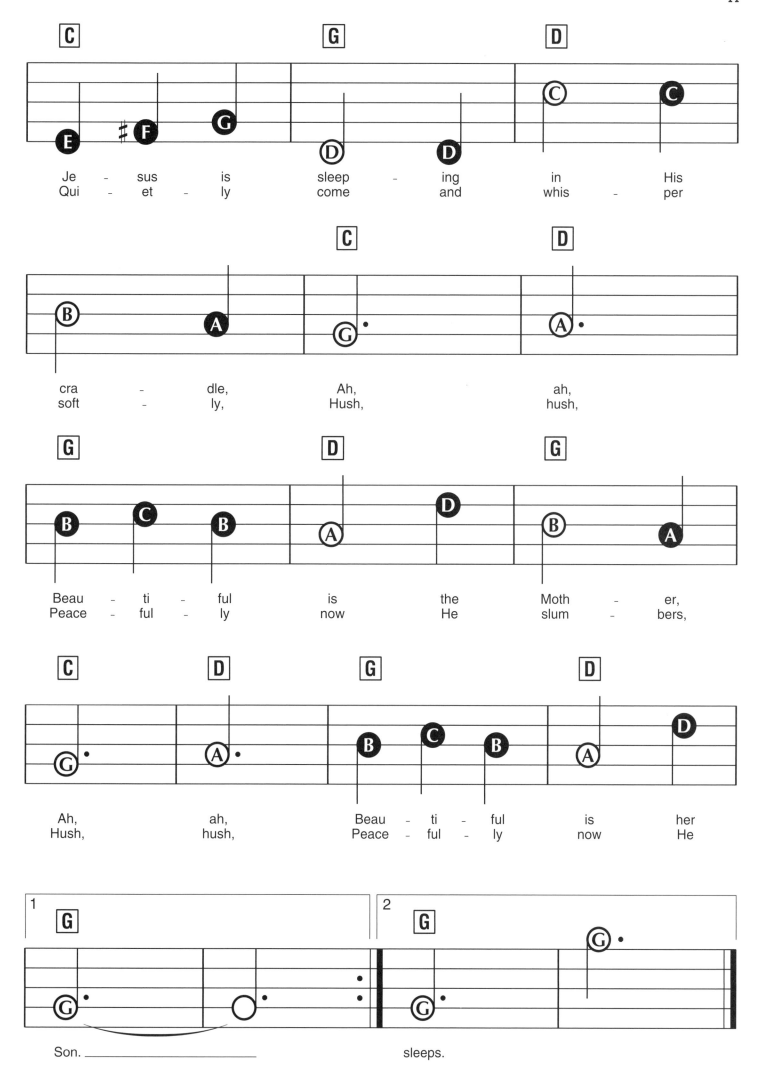

Come, Thou Long-Expected Jesus

Registration 1
Rhythm: Waltz

Words by Charles Wesley
Music by Rowland Hugh Prichard

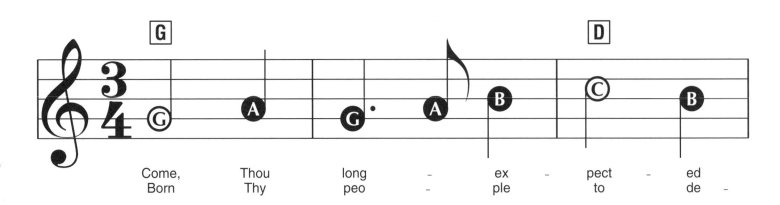

Come,   Thou   long   –   ex   –   pect   –   ed
Born   Thy   peo   –   ple   to   de   –

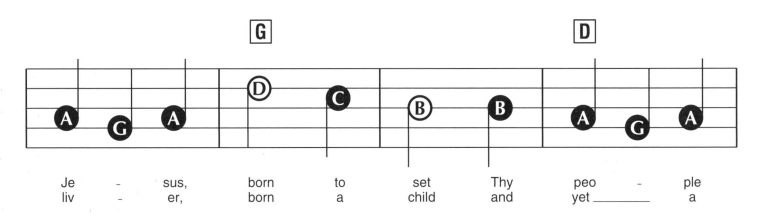

Je   –   sus,   born   to   set   Thy   peo   –   ple
liv   –   er,   born   born   a   child   and   yet _____   a

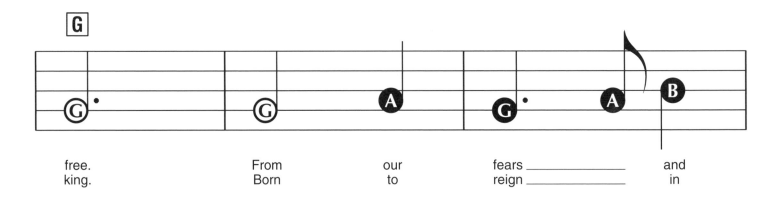

free.   From   our   fears _____   and
king.   Born   to   reign _____   in

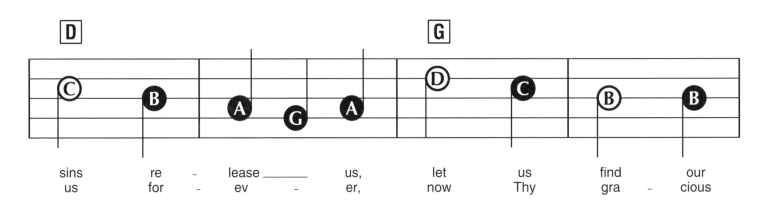

sins   re   –   lease _____   us,   let   us   find   our
us   for   –   ev   –   er,   now   Thy   gra   –   cious

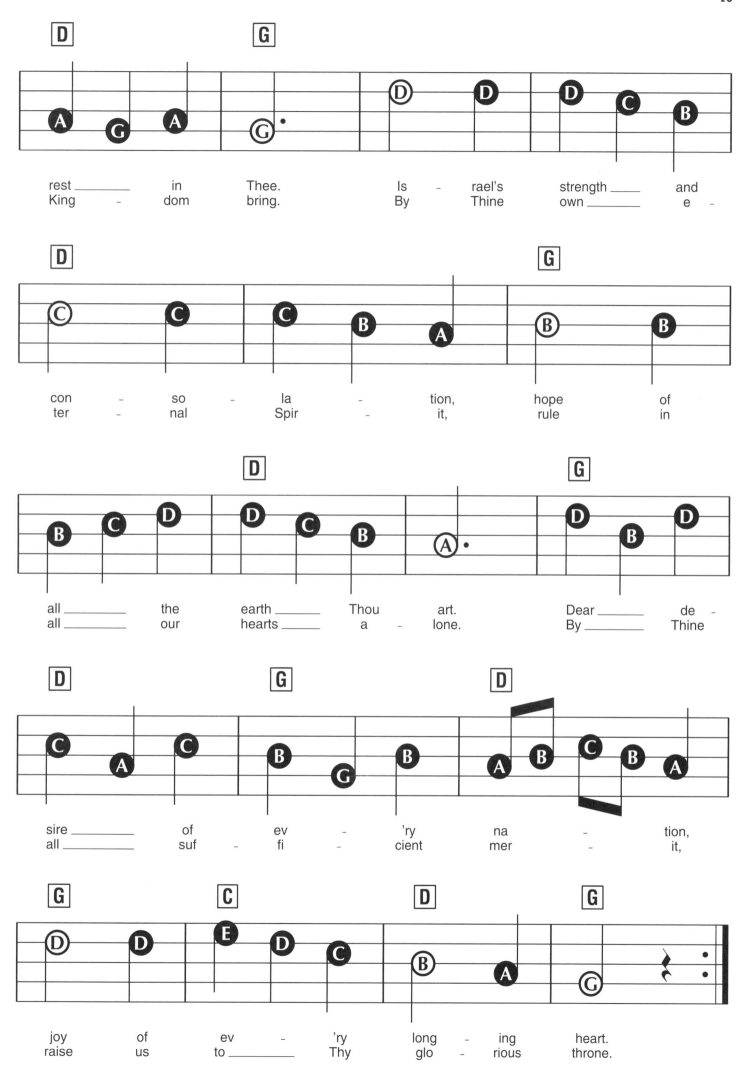

Ding Dong! Merrily on High!

Registration 5
Rhythm: March

French Carol

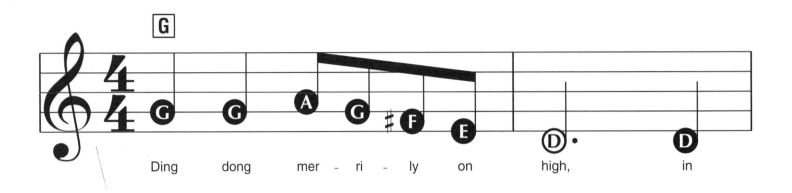

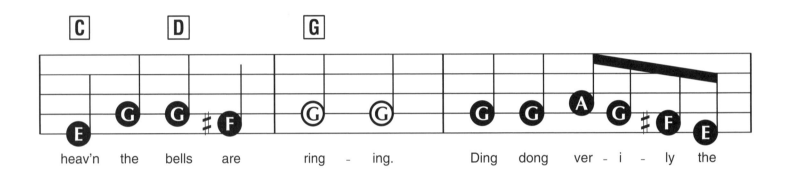

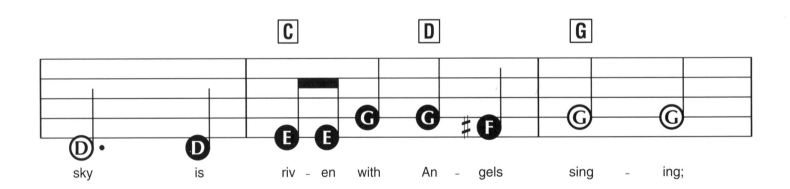

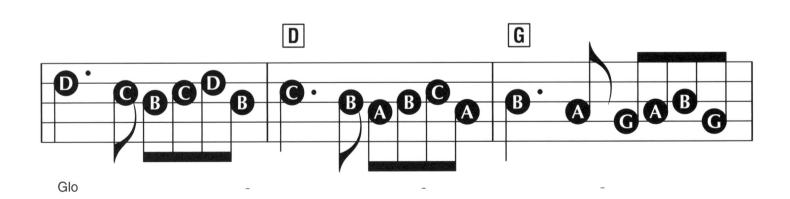

15

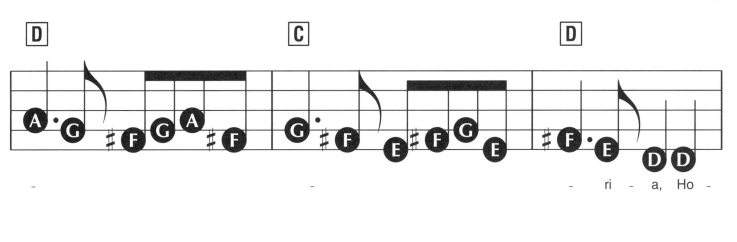

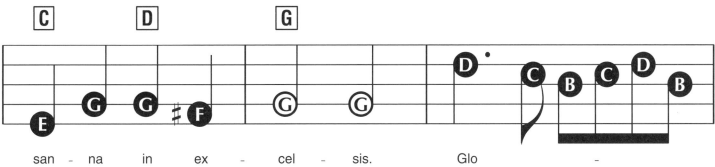

san - na in ex - cel - sis. Glo -

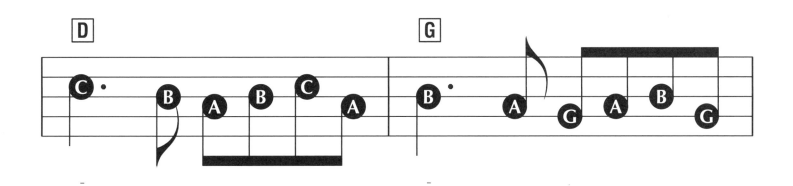

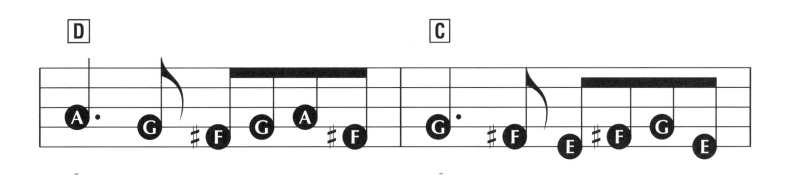

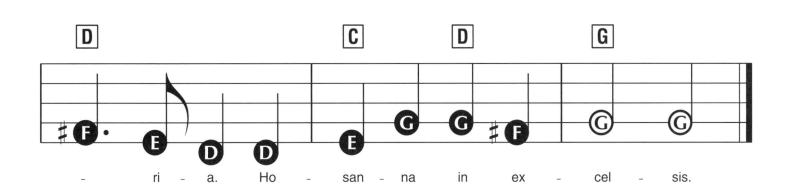

- ri - a. Ho - san - na in ex - cel - sis.

The First Noël

Registration 10
Rhythm: None

17th Century English Carol
Music from *W. Sandys' Christmas Carols*

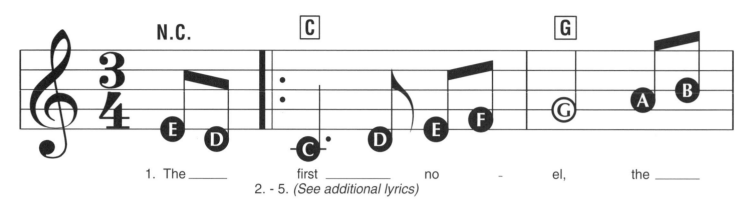

1. The _____ first _____ no - el, the _____
2. - 5. *(See additional lyrics)*

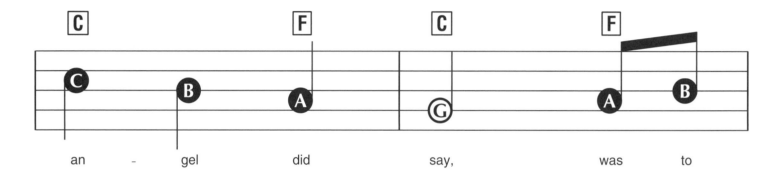

an - gel did say, was to

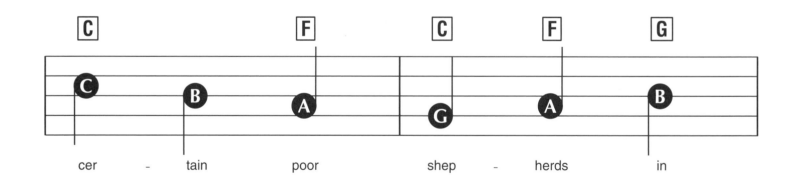

cer - tain poor shep - herds in

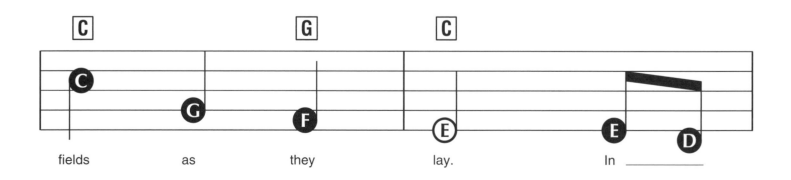

fields as they lay. In _____

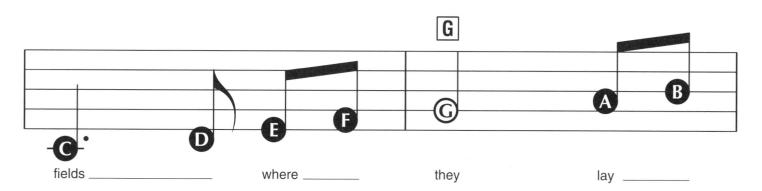

fields _____ where _____ they lay _____

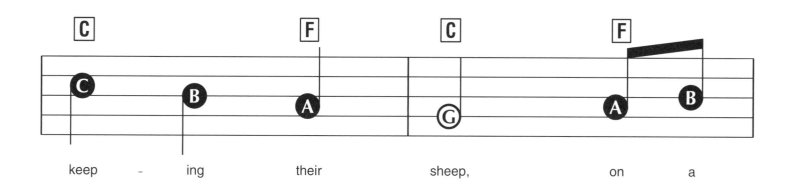

keep – ing their sheep, on a

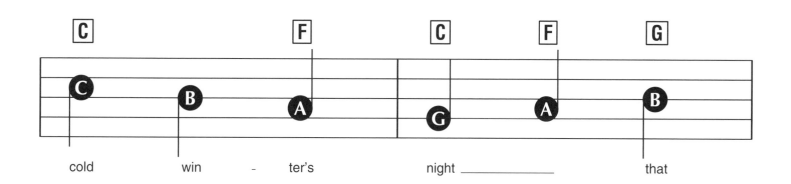

cold win – ter's night _____ that

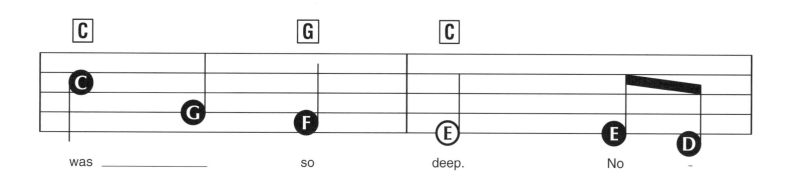

was _____ so deep. No –

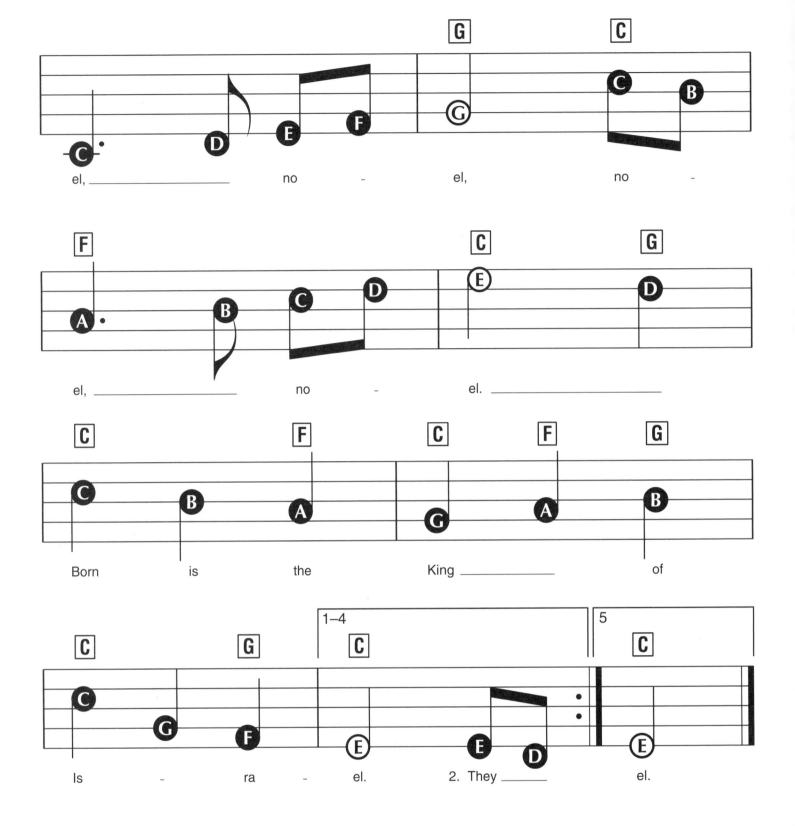

Additional Lyrics

2. They looked up and saw a star,
   Shining in the east, beyond them far.
   And to the earth it gave great light,
   And so it continued both day and night.
   Noel, noel, noel, noel.
   Born is the King of Israel.

3. And by the light of that same star,
   Three wisemen came from country far.
   To seek for a King was their intent,
   And to follow the star wherever it went.
   Noel, noel, noel, noel.
   Born is the King of Israel.

4. This star drew nigh to the northwest,
   O'er Bethlehem it took its rest.
   And there it did both stop and stay,
   Right over the place where Jesus lay.
   Noel, noel, noel, noel.
   Born is the King of Israel.

5. Then entered in those wisemen three,
   Full reverently upon the knee.
   And offered there, in His presence,
   Their gold, and myrrh, and frankincense.
   Noel, noel, noel, noel.
   Born is the King of Israel.

Good King Wenceslas

Registration 4
Rhythm: March

Words by John M. Neale
Music from *Piae Cantiones*

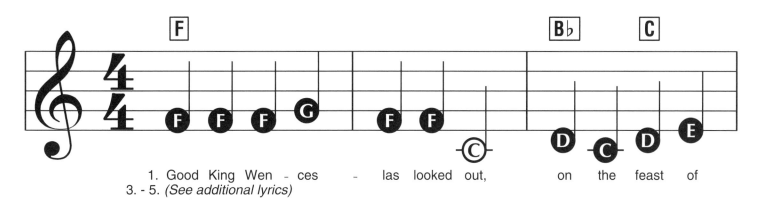

1. Good King Wen – ces – las looked out, on the feast of
3. - 5. *(See additional lyrics)*

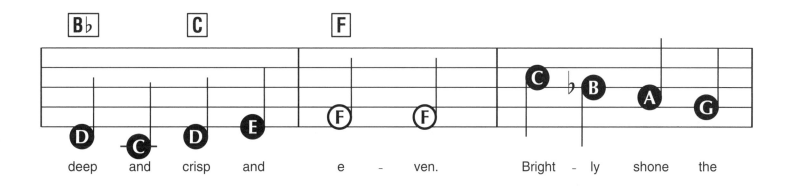

Ste – phen. When the snow lay 'round a – bout,

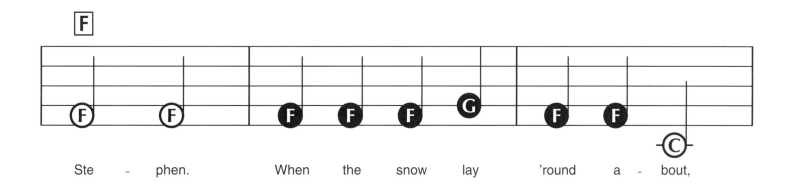

deep and crisp and e – ven. Bright – ly shone the

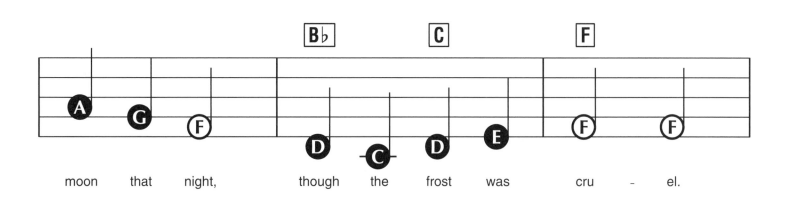

moon that night, though the frost was cru – el.

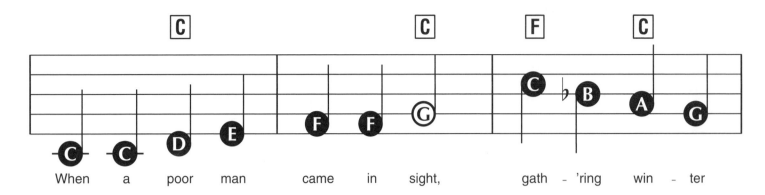

When a poor man came in sight, gath – 'ring win – ter

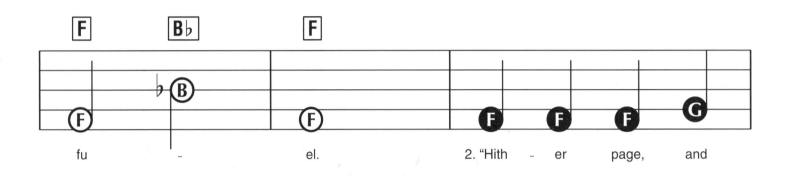

fu – el. 2. "Hith – er page, and

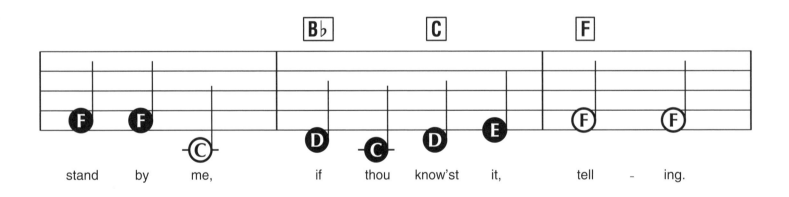

stand by me, if thou know'st it, tell – ing.

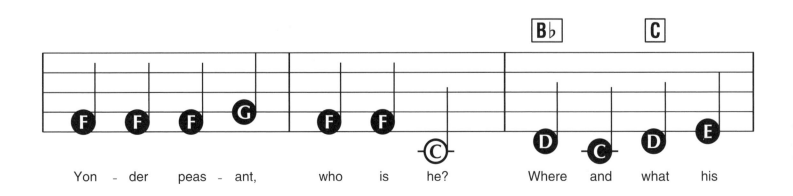

Yon – der peas – ant, who is he? Where and what his

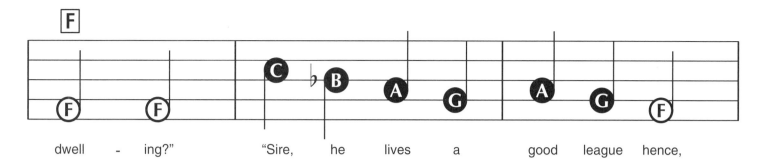

dwell - ing?" "Sire, he lives a good league hence,

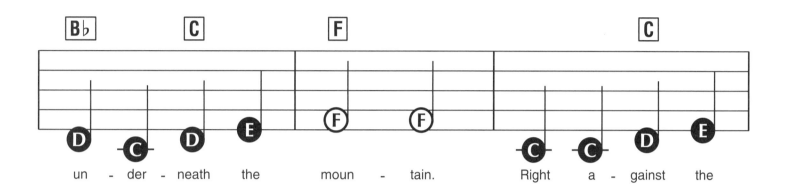

un - der - neath the moun - tain. Right a - gainst the

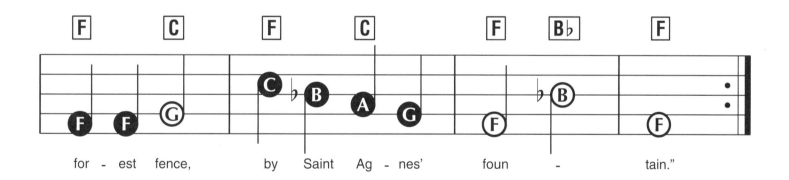

for - est fence, by Saint Ag - nes' foun - tain."

Additional Lyrics

3. "Bring me flesh, and bring me wine,
   Bring me pine-logs hither.
   Thou and I will see him dine,
   When we bear them thither."
   Page and monarch forth they went,
   Forth they went together.
   Through the rude winds wild lament,
   And the bitter weather.

4. "Sire, the night is darker now,
   And the wind blows stronger.
   Fails my heart, I know not how,
   I can go not longer."
   "Mark my footsteps, my good page,
   Tread thou in them boldly.
   Thou shalt find the winter's rage,
   Freeze thy blood less coldly."

5. In his master's steps he trod,
   Where the snow lay dinted.
   Heat was in the very sod,
   Which the saint had printed.
   Therefore, Christian men, be sure,
   Wealth or rank possessing.
   Ye who now will bless the poor,
   Shall yourselves find blessing.

The Friendly Beasts

Registration 1
Rhythm: Waltz

Traditional English Carol

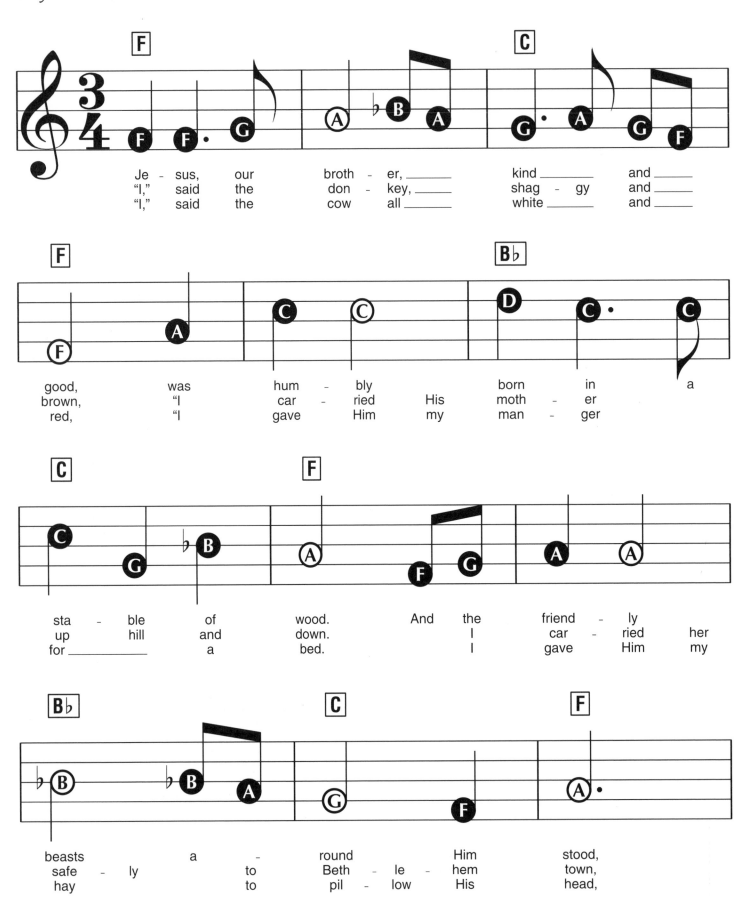

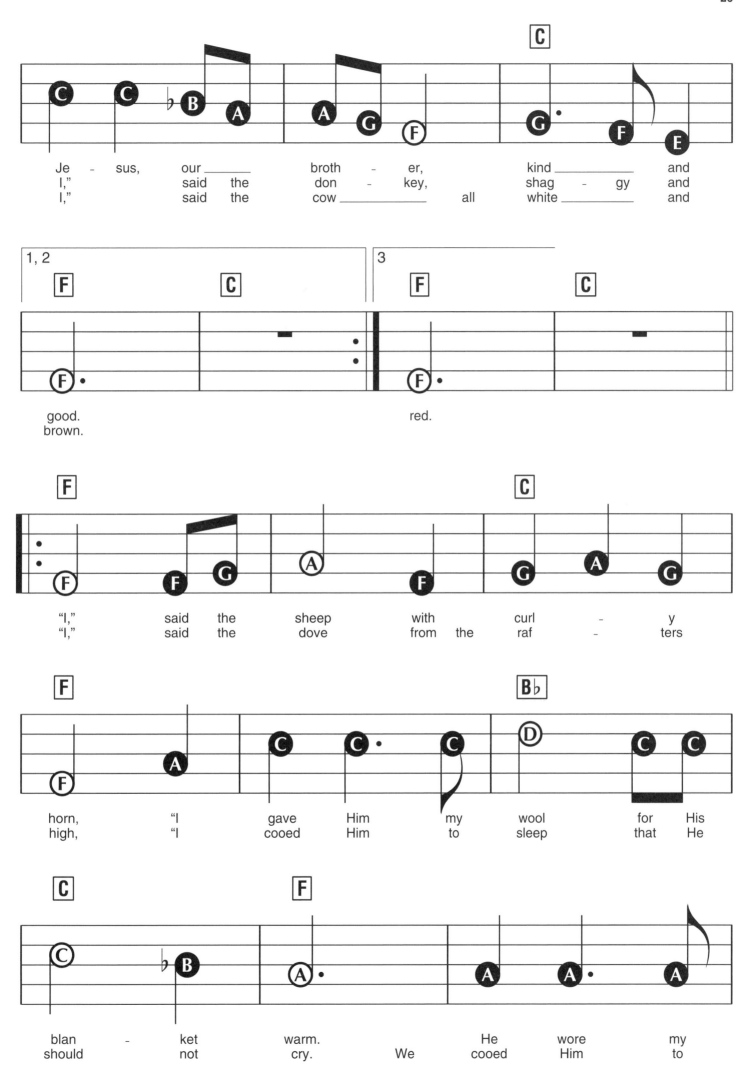

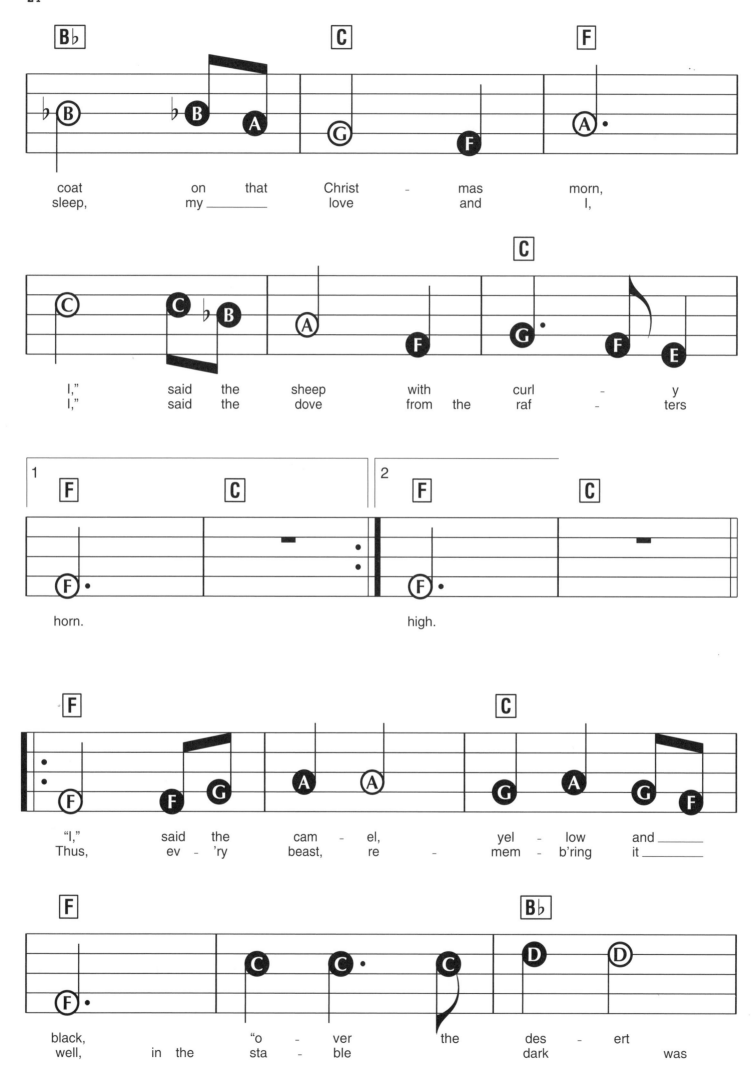

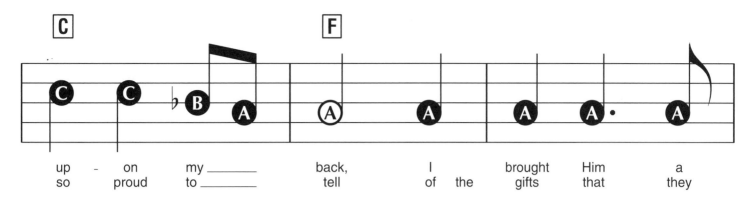

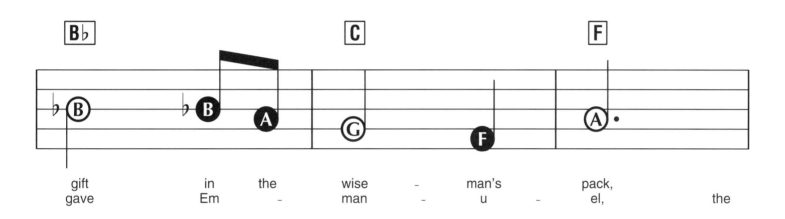

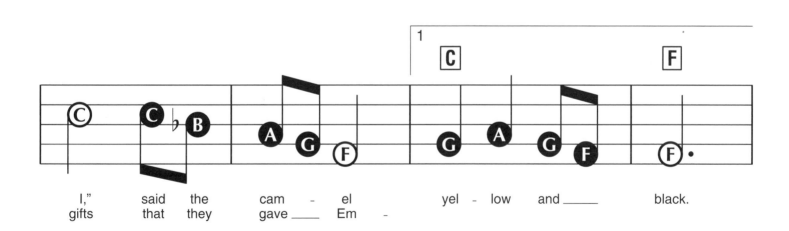

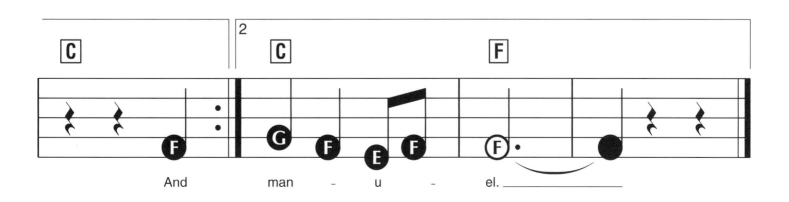

Go, Tell It on the Mountain

Registration 5
Rhythm: Swing

African-American Spiritual
Verses by John W. Work, Jr.

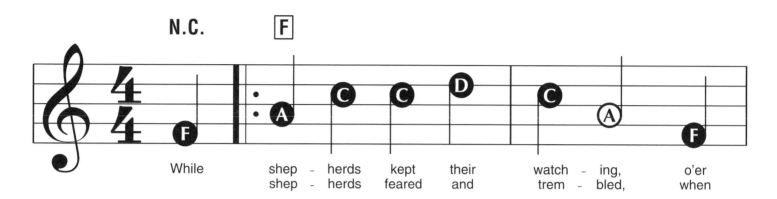

While shep - herds kept their watch - ing, o'er
shep - herds feared and trem - bled, when

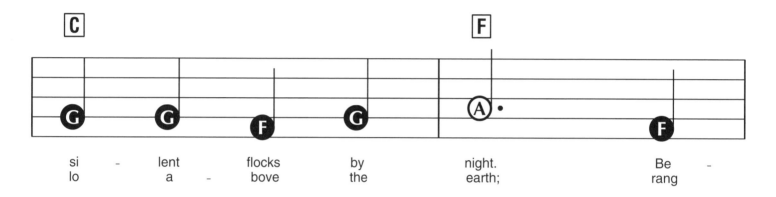

si - lent flocks by night. Be -
lo a - bove the earth; rang

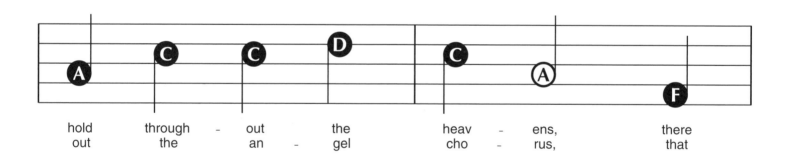

hold through - out the heav - ens, there
out the an - gel cho - rus, that

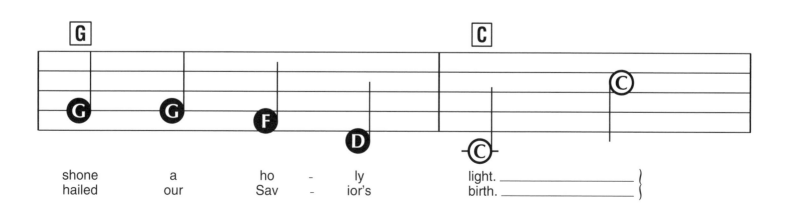

shone a ho - ly light. ____
hailed our Sav - ior's birth. ____

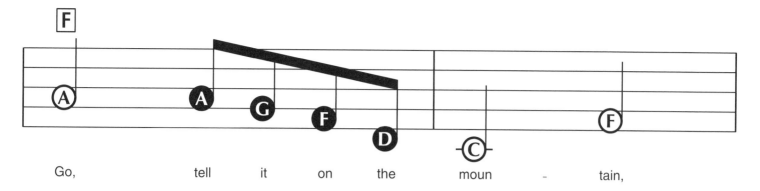

Go, tell it on the moun – tain,

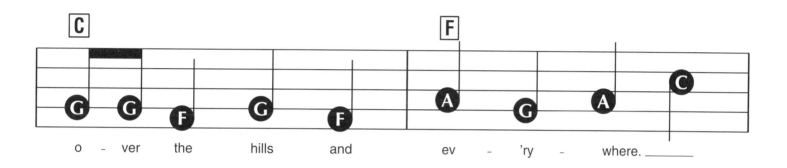

o – ver the hills and ev – 'ry – where. _____

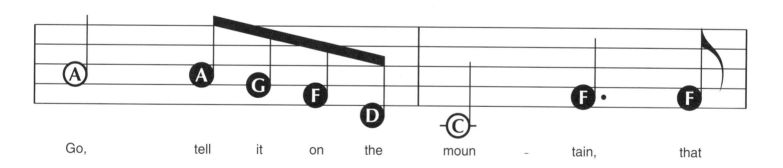

Go, tell it on the moun – tain, that

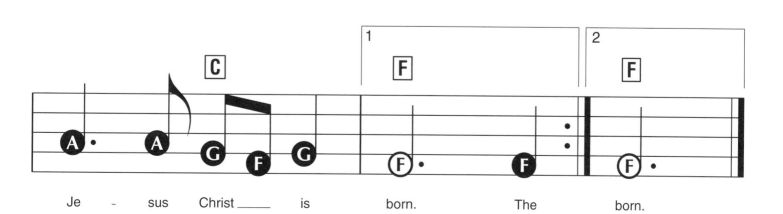

Je – sus Christ _____ is born. The born.

Hark! The Herald Angels Sing

Registration 7
Rhythm: None

Words by Charles Wesley
Altered by George Whitefield
Music by Felix Mendelssohn-Bartholdy
Arranged by William H. Cummings

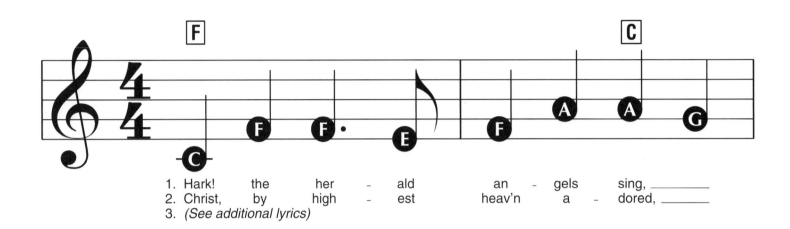

1. Hark! the her - ald an - gels sing, _____
2. Christ, by high - est heav'n a - dored, _____
3. *(See additional lyrics)*

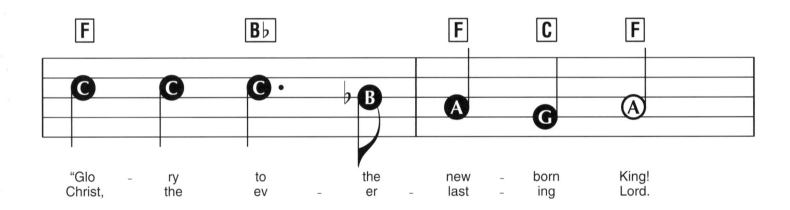

"Glo - ry to the new - born King!
Christ, ry the ev - er - last - ing King Lord.

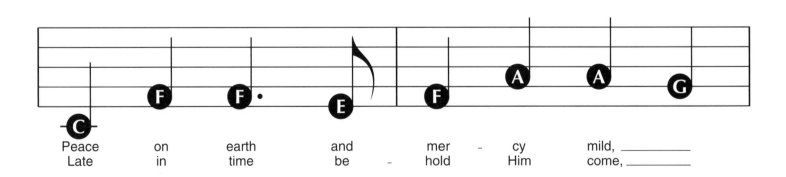

Peace on earth and mer - cy mild, _____
Late in time be - hold Him come, _____

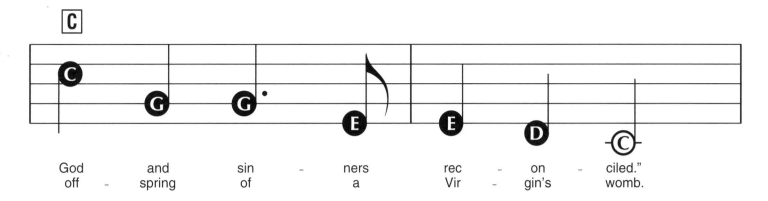

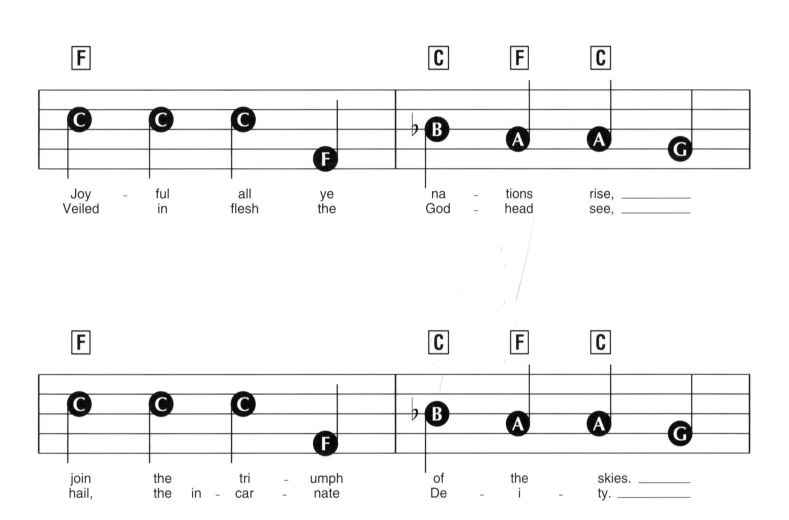

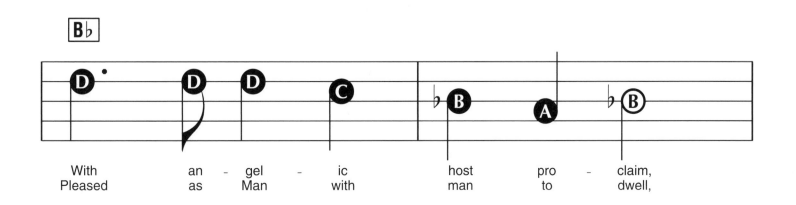

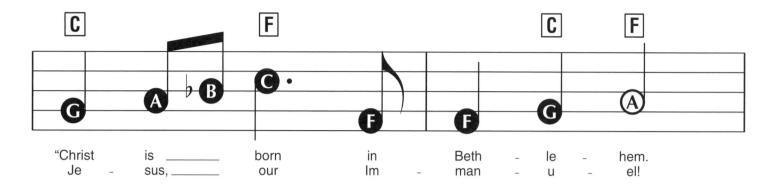

"Christ   is _____ born   in   Beth – le – hem.
Je – sus, _____ our   Im – man – u – el!

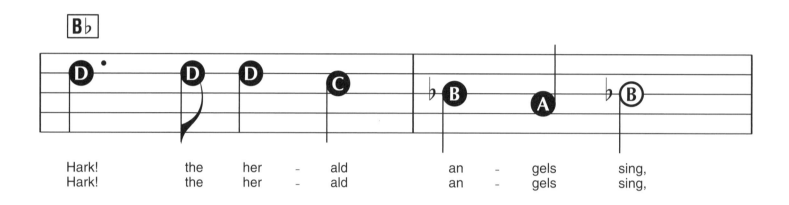

Hark!   the   her – ald   an – gels   sing,
Hark!   the   her – ald   an – gels   sing,

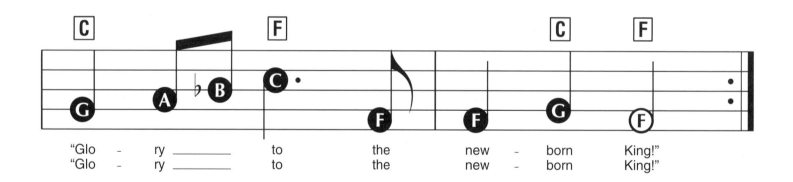

"Glo – ry _____ to   the   new – born   King!"
"Glo – ry _____ to   the   new – born   King!"

Additional Lyrics

3. Hail, the heaven-born Prince of Peace!
Hail, the Sun of Righteousness!
Light and life to all He brings,
Risen with healing in His wings.
Mild He lays His glory by,
Born that man no more may die.
Born to raise the sons of earth,
Born to give them second birth.

Hark! the herald angels sing,
"Glory to the newborn King!"

Jingle Bells

Registration 5
Rhythm: Fox Trot or Swing

Words and Music by
J. Pierpont

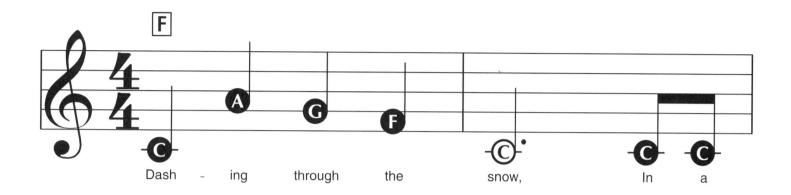

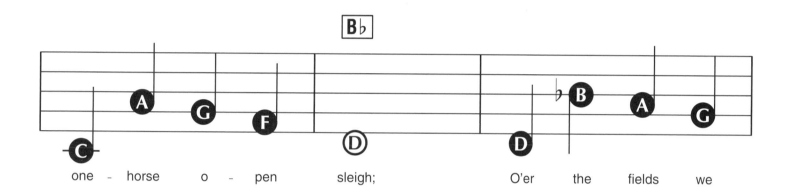

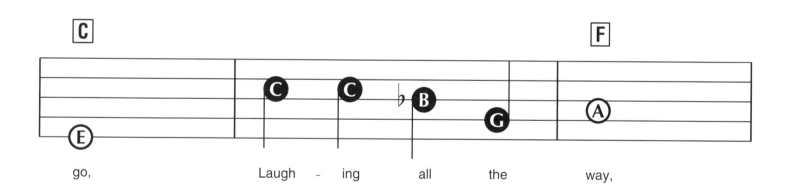

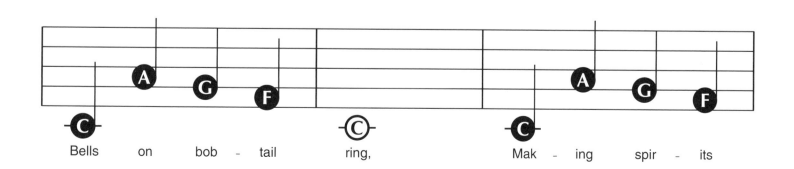

32

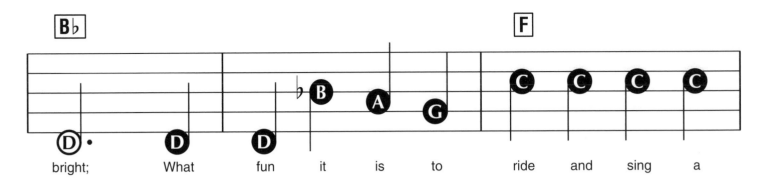

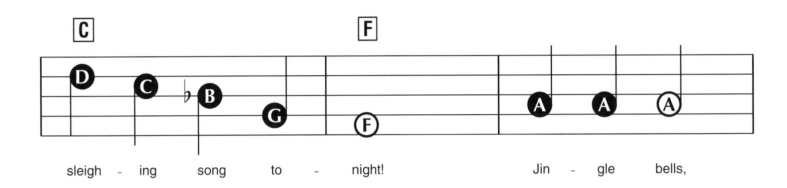

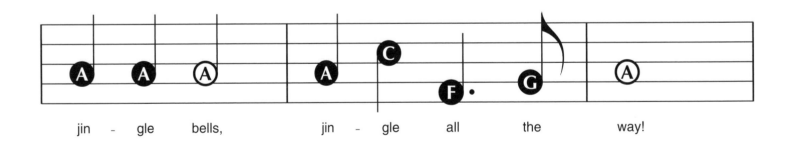

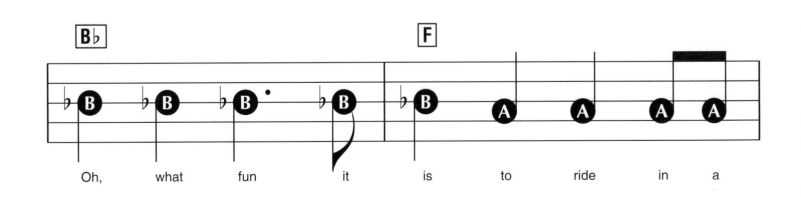

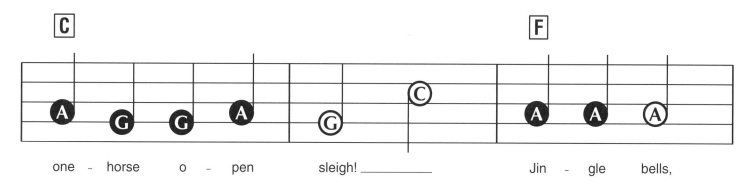

one - horse o - pen sleigh! _____ Jin - gle bells,

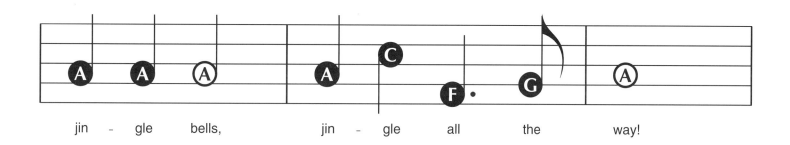

jin - gle bells, jin - gle all the way!

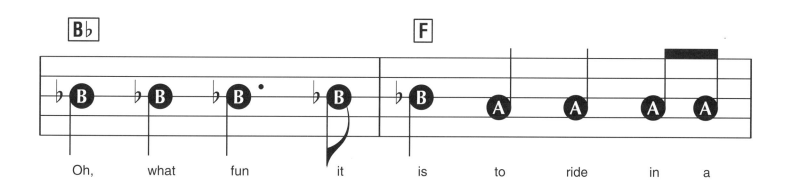

Oh, what fun it is to ride in a

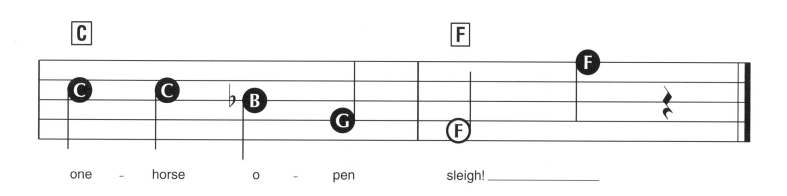

one - horse o - pen sleigh! _____

He Is Born, the Holy Child
(Il Est Ne, Le Divin Enfant)

Registration 3
Rhythm: None

Traditional French Carol

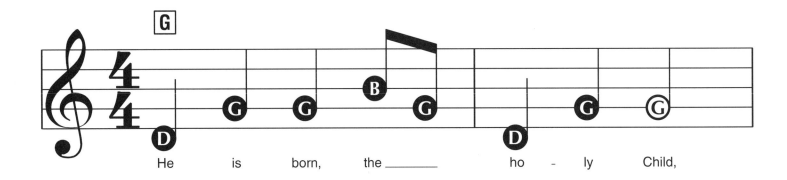

He is born, the _____ ho - ly Child,

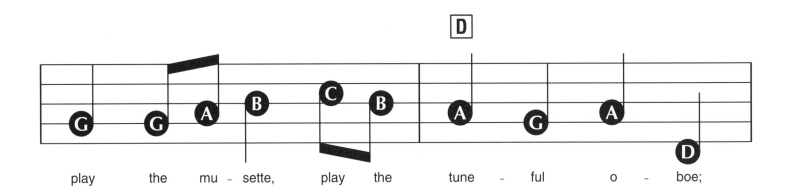

play the mu - sette, play the tune - ful o - boe;

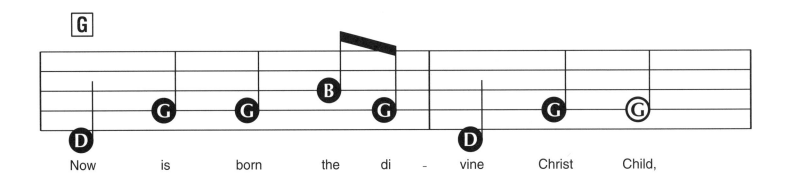

Now is born the di - vine Christ Child,

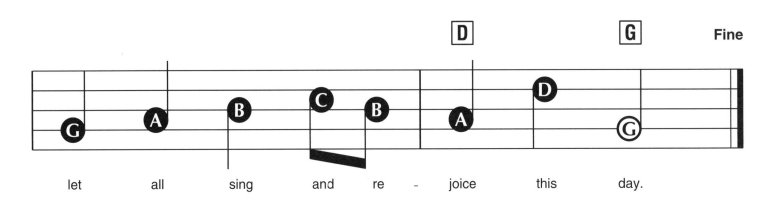

let all sing and re - joice this day.

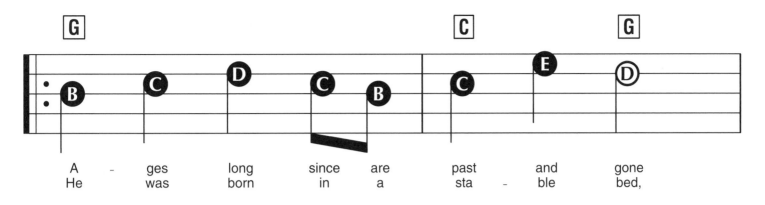

A - ges long since are past and gone
He was long born in a sta - ble bed,

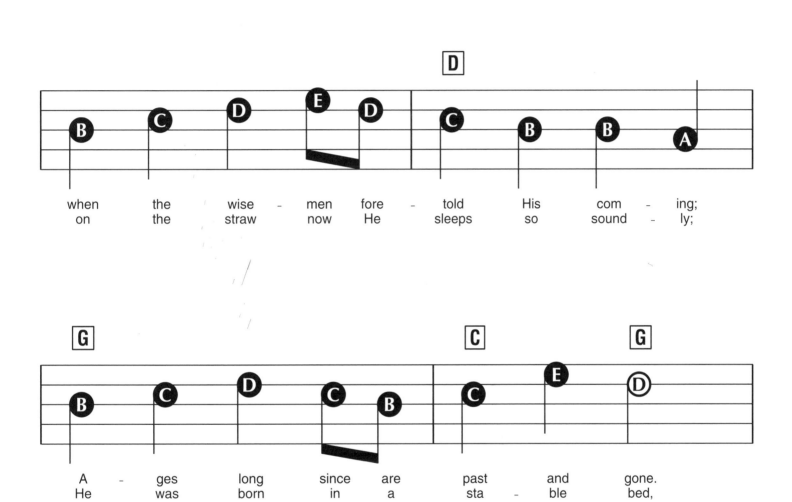

when the wise - men fore - told His com - ing;
on the straw now He sleeps so sound - ly;

A - ges long since are past and gone.
He was long born in a sta - ble bed,

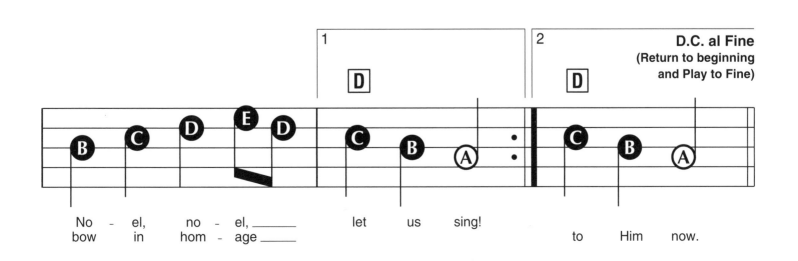

No - el, no - el,_____ let us sing!
bow in hom - age _____ to Him now.

D.C. al Fine
(Return to beginning
and Play to Fine)

Here We Come A-Wassailing

Registration 3
Rhythm: 6/8 March

Traditional

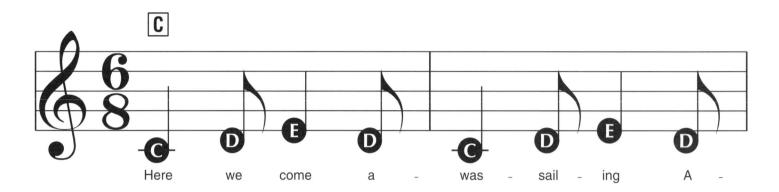

Here we come a - was - sail - ing A -

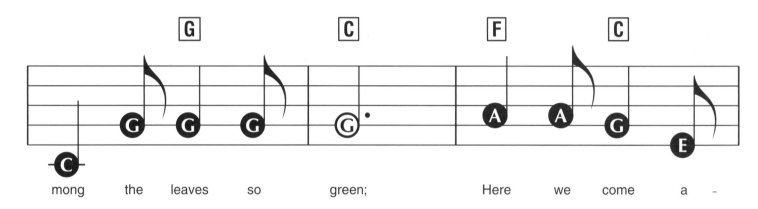

mong the leaves so green; Here we come a -

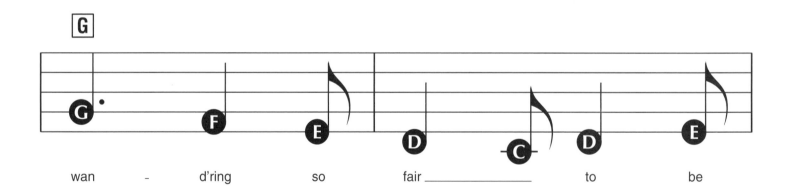

wan - d'ring so fair _____ to be

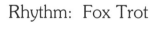

Rhythm: Fox Trot

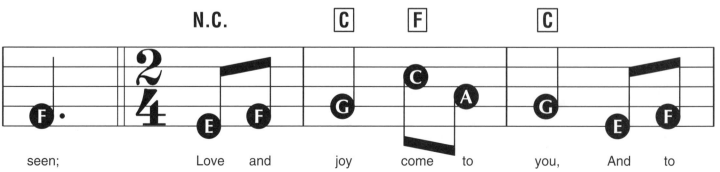

seen; Love and joy come to you, And to

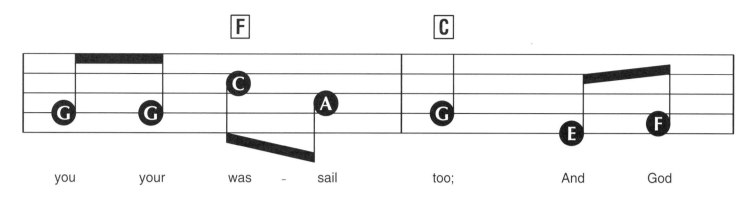

you   your   was - sail   too;   And   God

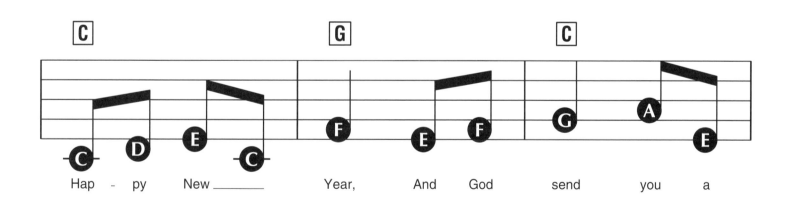

bless   you,   and   send _____ you   a

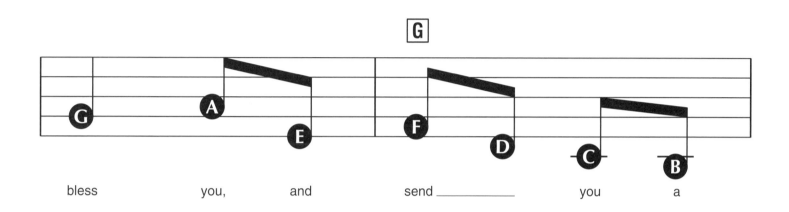

Hap - py New _____ Year,   And   God   send   you   a

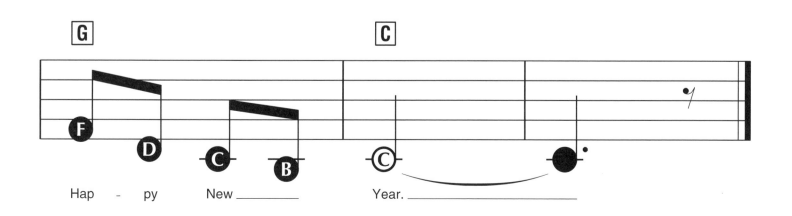

Hap - py   New _____   Year. _____

I Saw Three Ships

Registration 2
Rhythm: 6/8 March

Traditional English Carol

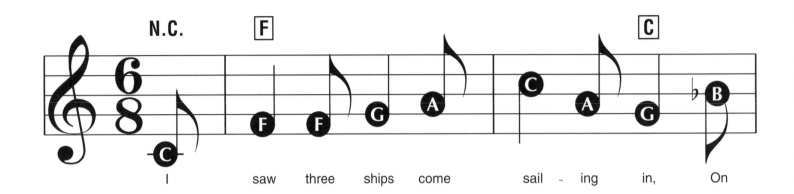

I saw three ships come sail - ing in, On

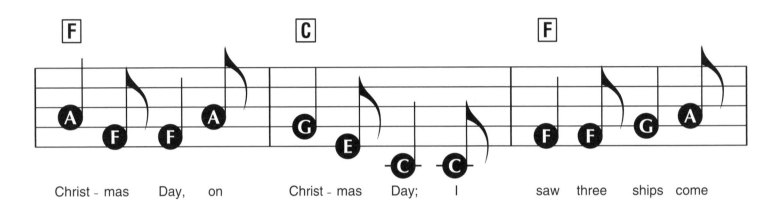

Christ - mas Day, on Christ - mas Day; I saw three ships come

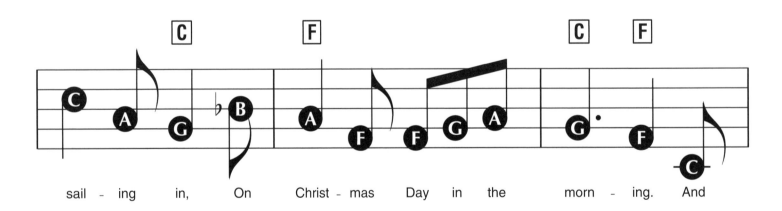

sail - ing in, On Christ - mas Day in the morn - ing. And

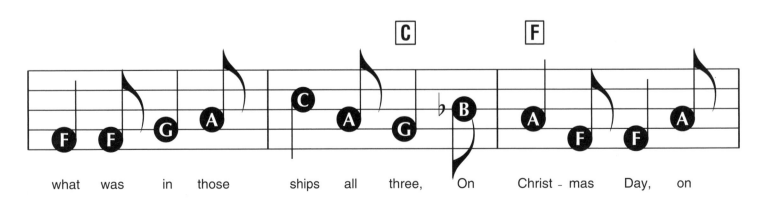

what was in those ships all three, On Christ - mas Day, on

Infant Holy, Infant Lowly

Registration 4
Rhythm: Waltz

Traditional Polish Carol
Paraphrased by Edith M.G. Reed

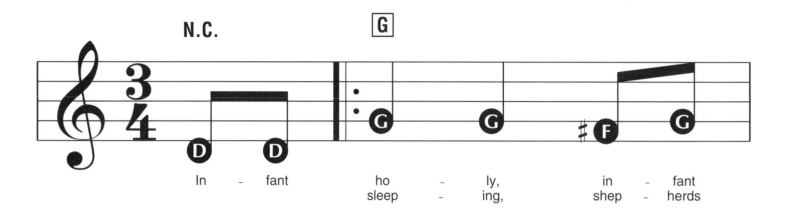

In - fant ho - ly, in - fant
sleep - ing, in shep - herds

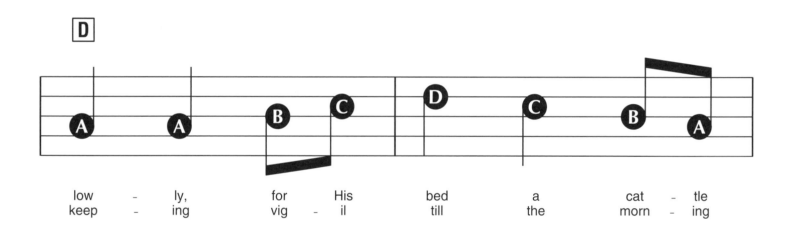

low - ly, for His bed a cat - tle
keep - ing vig - il till the morn - ing

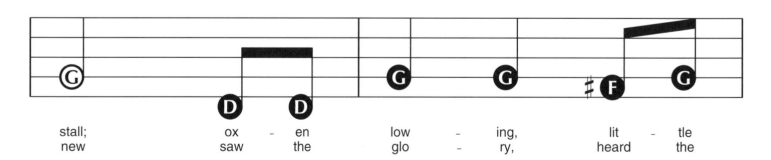

stall; ox - en low - ing, lit - tle
new saw the glo - ry, heard the

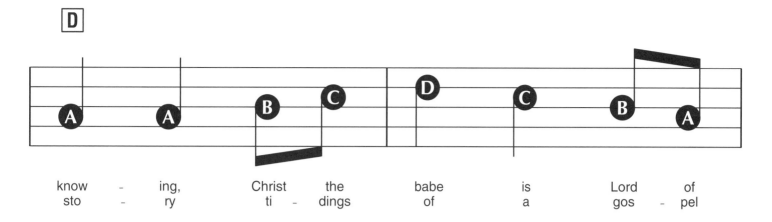

know - ing, Christ the babe is Lord of
sto - ry ti - dings of a Lord gos - pel

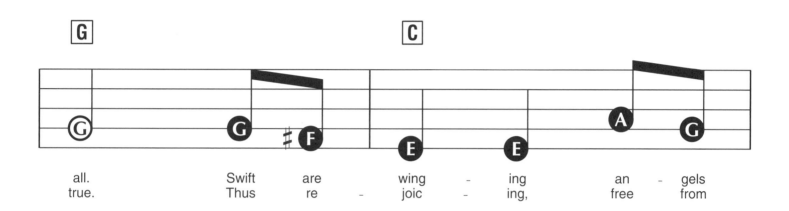

all. Swift are wing - ing an - gels
true. Thus re - joic - ing, free from

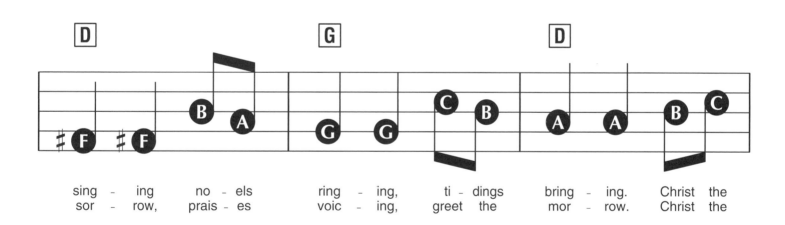

sing - ing no - els ring - ing, ti - dings bring - ing. Christ the
sor - row, prais - es voic - ing, greet the mor - row. Christ the

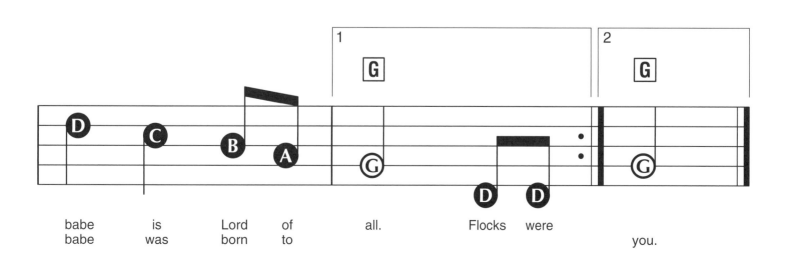

babe is Lord of all. Flocks were
babe is was born to you.

Joy to the World

Registration 2
Rhythm: March

Words by Isaac Watts
Music by George Frideric Handel
Arranged by Lowell Mason

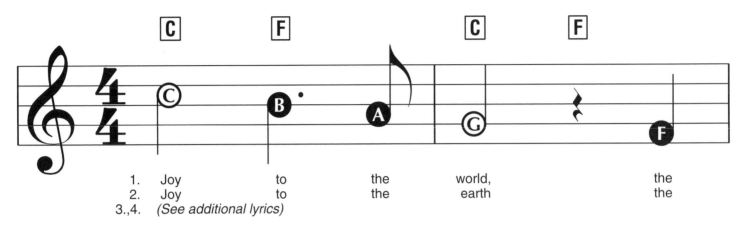

1. Joy   to   the   world,   the
2. Joy   to   the   earth   the
3.,4. *(See additional lyrics)*

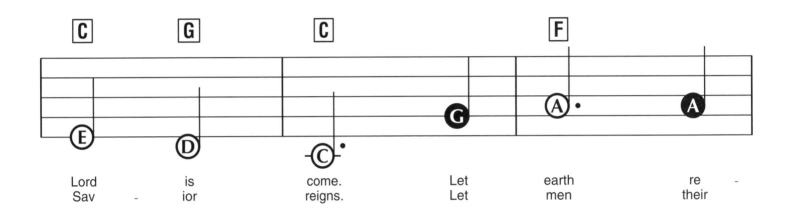

Lord   is   come.   Let   earth   re -
Sav -   ior   reigns.   Let   men   their

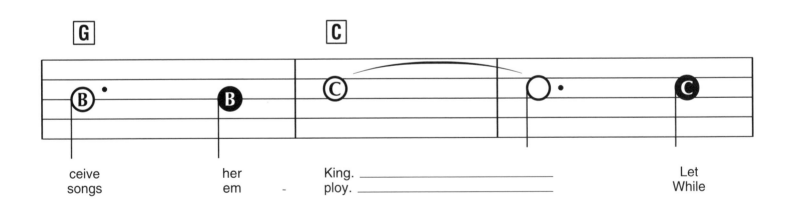

ceive   her   King. _____   Let
songs   em -   ploy. _____   While

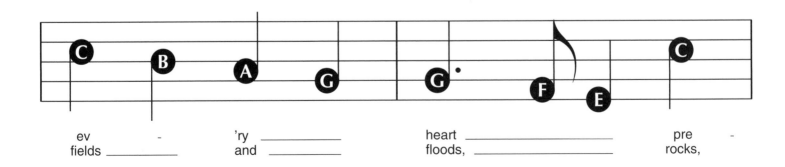

ev -   'ry _____   heart _____   pre -
fields _____   and _____   floods, _____   rocks,

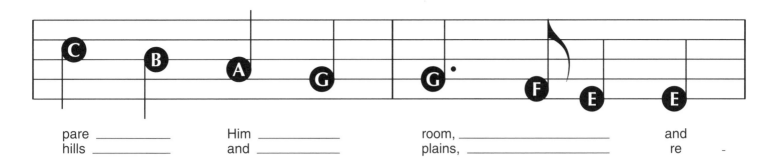

pare _____ Him _____ room, _____ and
hills _____ and _____ plains, _____ re -

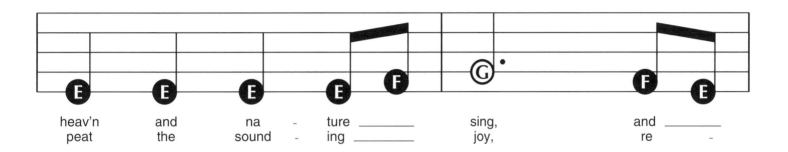

heav'n   and   na - ture _____ sing,   and _____
peat   the   sound - ing _____ joy,   re   -

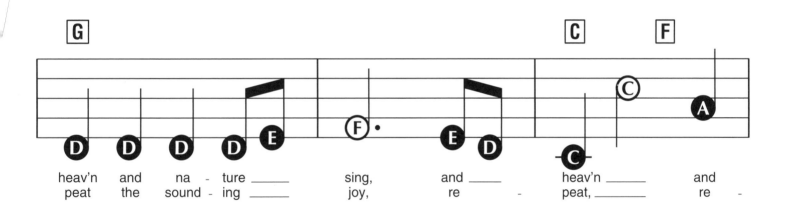

heav'n   and   na - ture _____   sing,   and _____   heav'n _____   and
peat   the   sound - ing _____   joy,   re   -   peat, _____   re   -

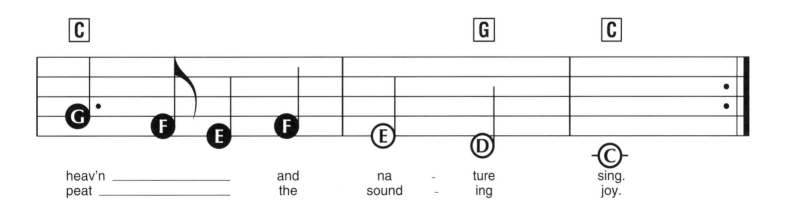

heav'n _____ and   na - ture   sing.
peat _____ the   sound - ing   joy.

Additional Lyrics

3. No more let sins and sorrows grow,
   Nor thorns infest the ground.
   He comes to make His blessings flow,
   Far as the curse is found,
   Far as the curse is found,
   Far as, far as the curse is found.

4. He rules the world with truth and grace,
   And makes the nations prove;
   The glories of His righteousness,
   And wonders of His love,
   And wonders of His love,
   And wonders, wonders of His love.

Mary Had a Baby

Registration 2
Rhythm: Calypso or Latin

African-American Spiritual

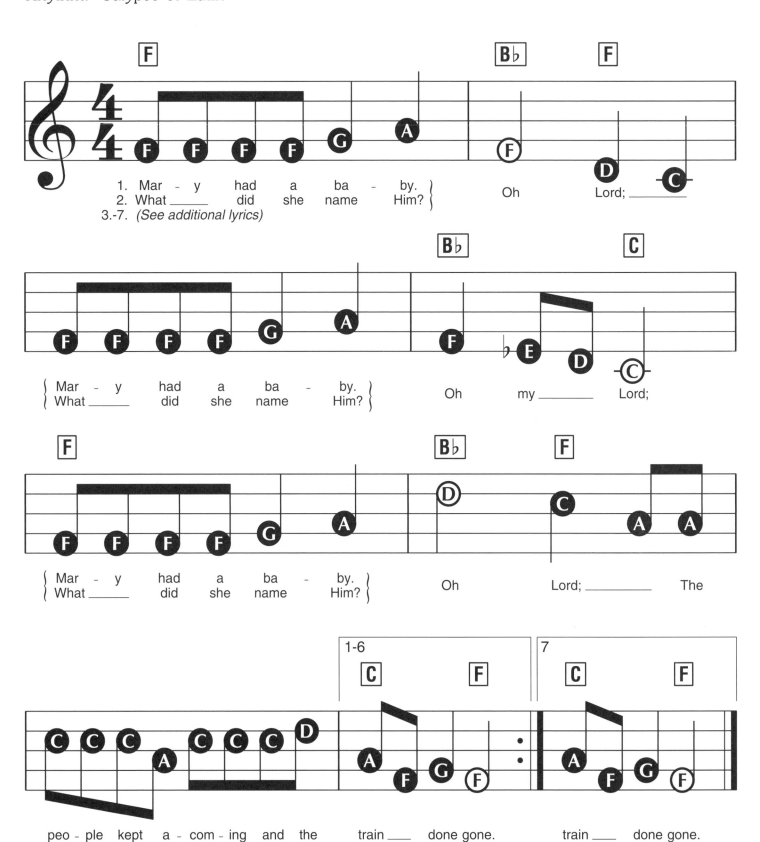

Additional Lyrics

3. She called Him Jesus.
4. Where was He born?
5. Born in a stable.

6. Where did they lay Him?
7. Laid Him in a manger.

O Christmas Tree

Registration 3
Rhythm: None

Traditional German Carol

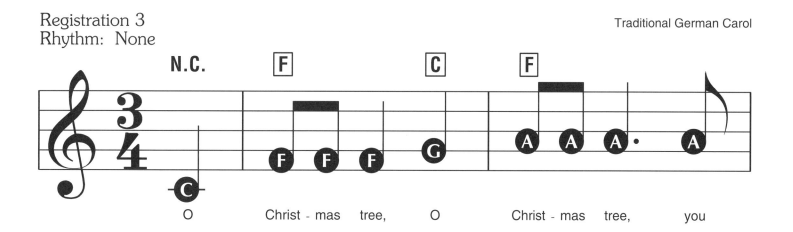

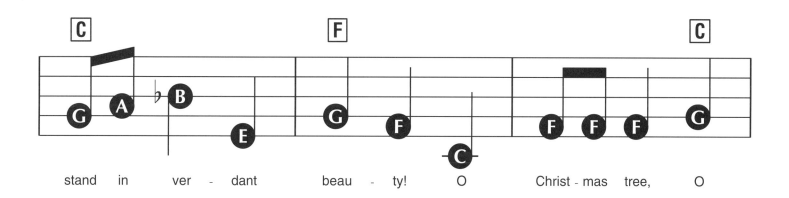

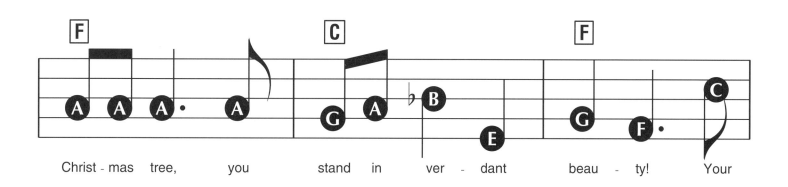

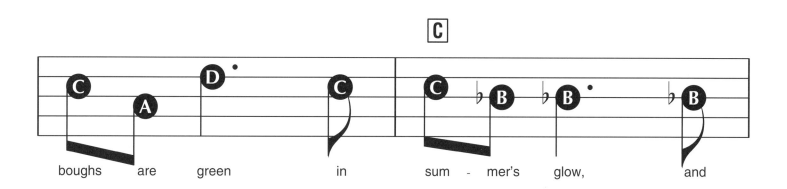

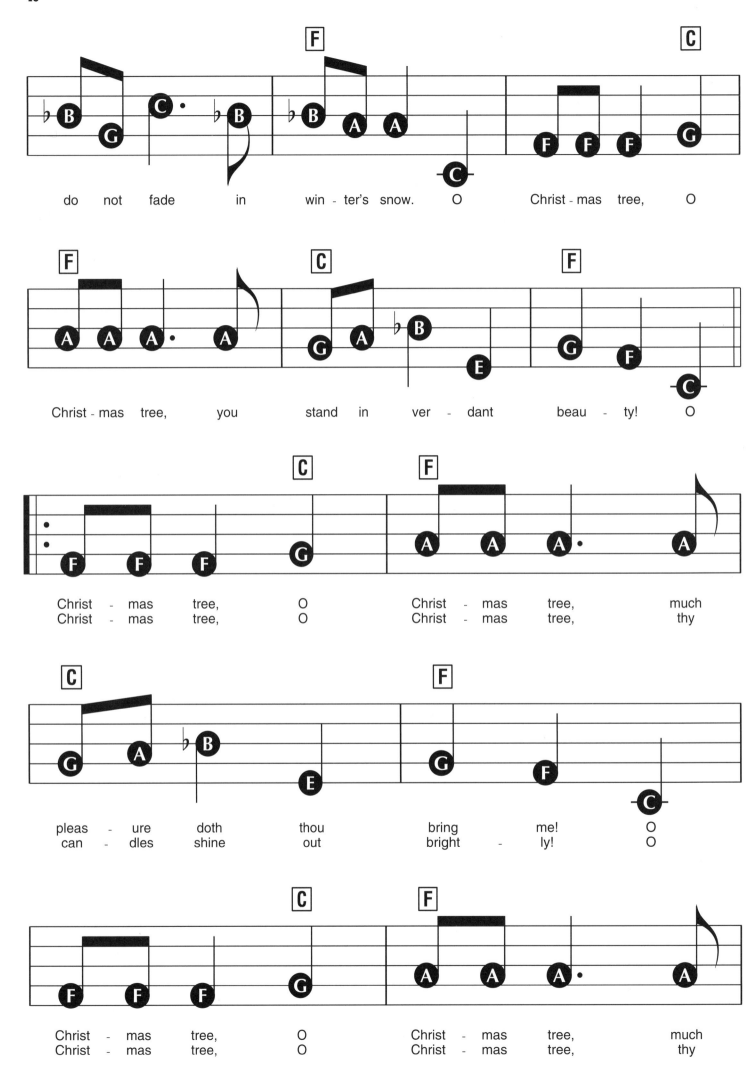

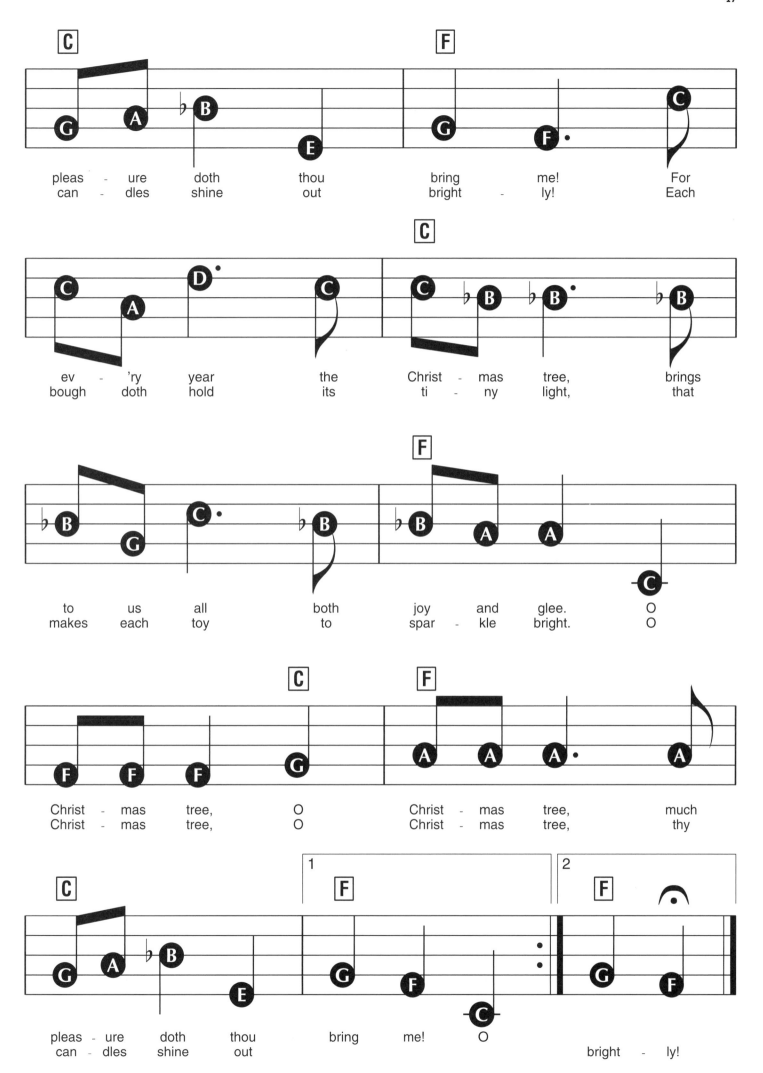

O Come, All Ye Faithful
(Adeste Fideles)

Registration 1
Rhythm: March

Words and Music by John Francis Wade
Latin Words translated by Frederick Oakeley

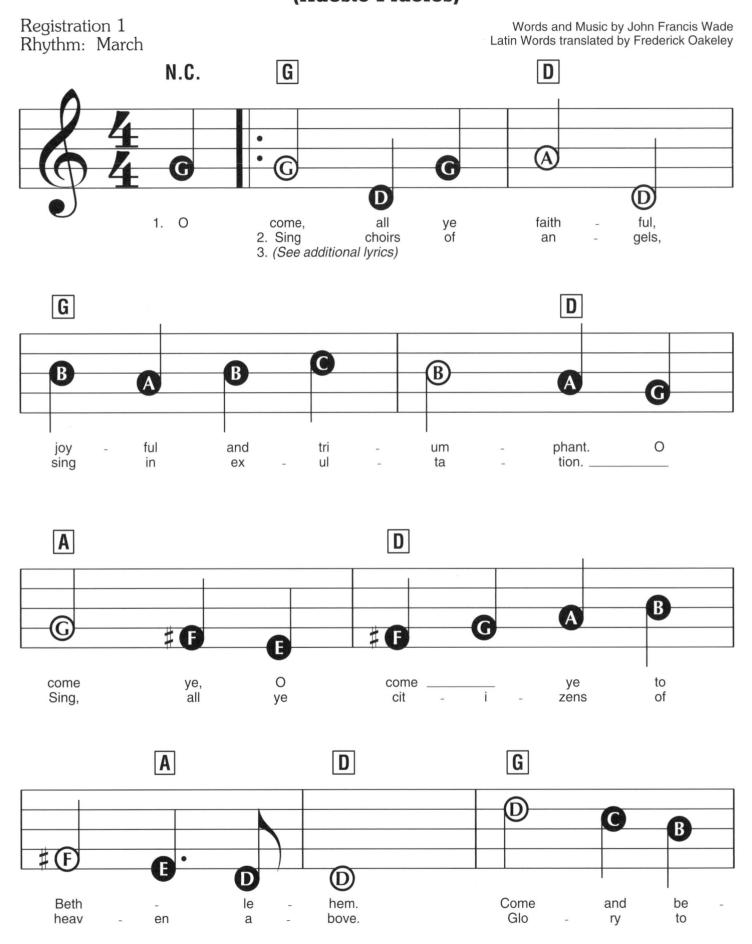

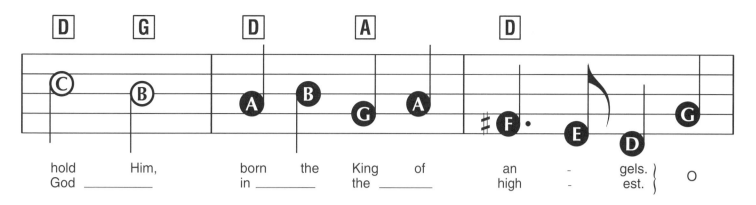

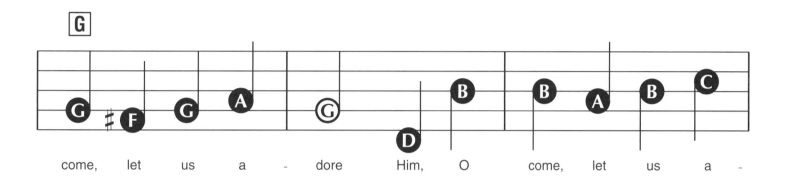

hold Him, born the King of an - gels. } O
God _____ in _____ the _____ high - est. }

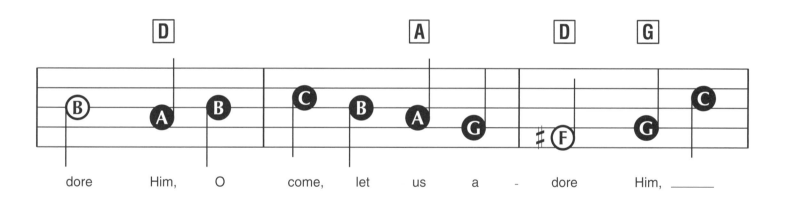

come, let us a - dore Him, O come, let us a -

dore Him, O come, let us a - dore Him, _____

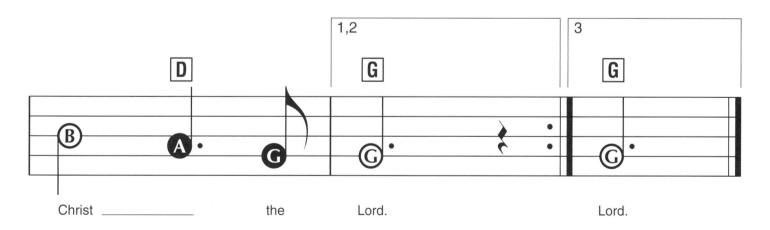

Christ _____ the Lord. Lord.

Additional Lyrics

3. Yea, Lord we greet Thee, born this happy morning.
   Jesus, to Thee be glory given.
   Word of the Father, now in flesh appearing.
   O come let us adore Him, O come let us adore Him.
   O come let us adore Him, Christ the Lord.

O Come, Little Children

Registration 1
Rhythm: 4/4 Ballad

Words by C. von Schmidt
Music by J.P.A. Schulz

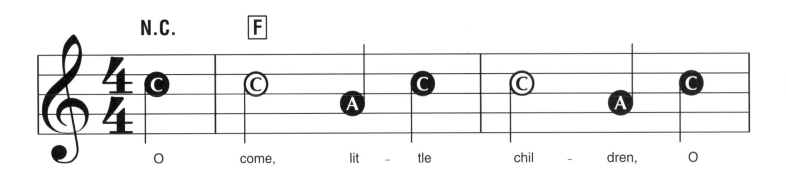

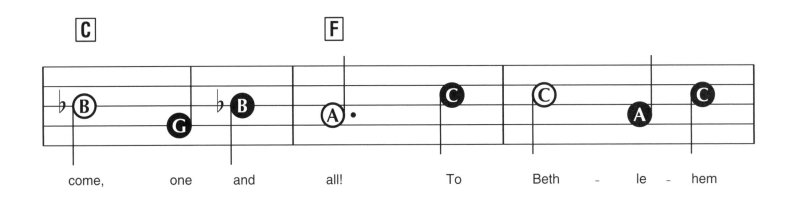

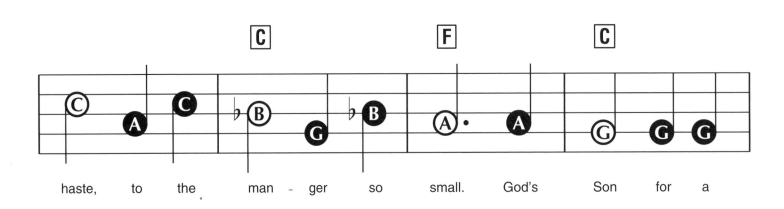

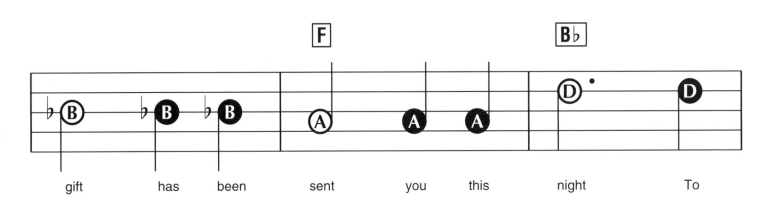

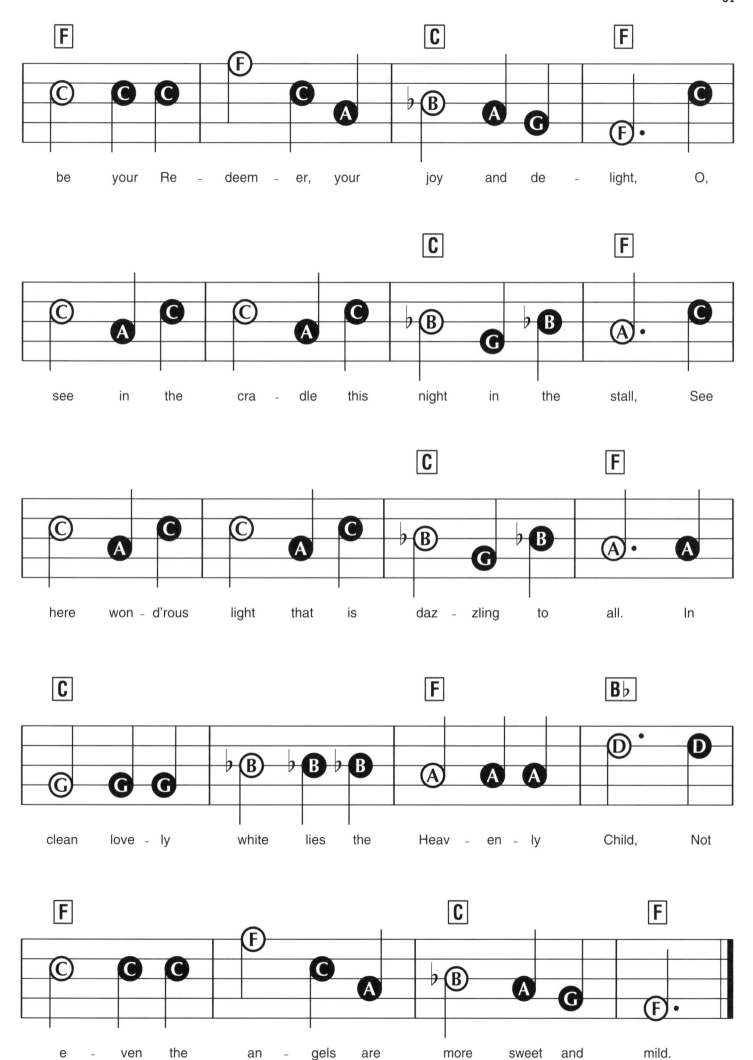

Silent Night

Registration 1
Rhythm: Waltz

Words by Joseph Mohr
Translated by John F. Young
Music by Franz X. Gruber

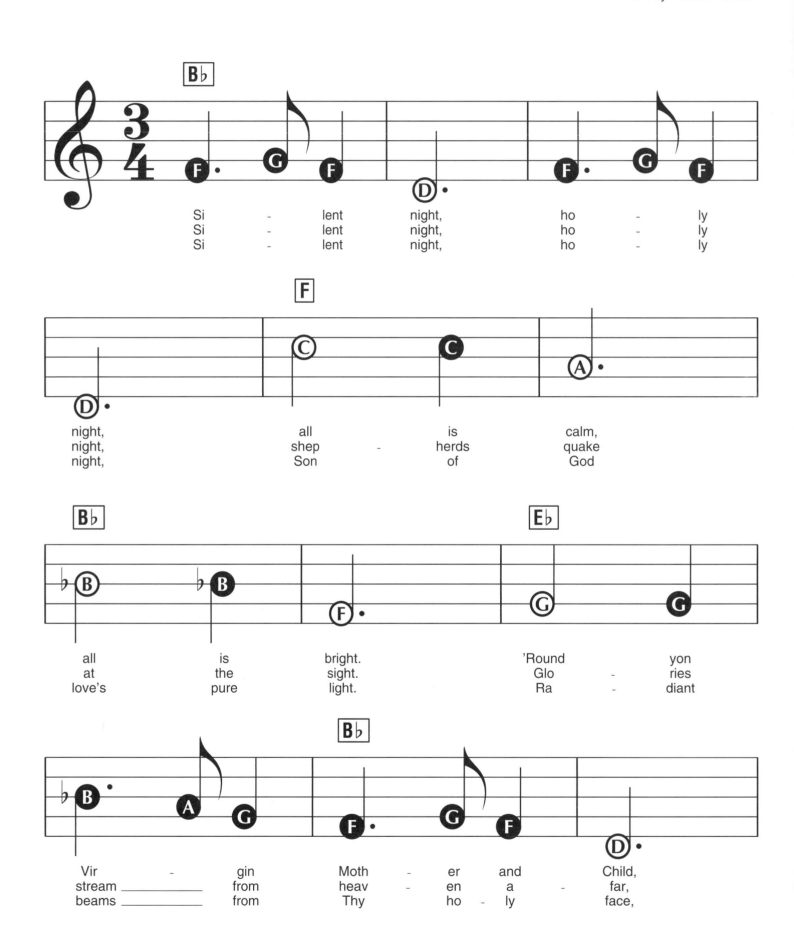

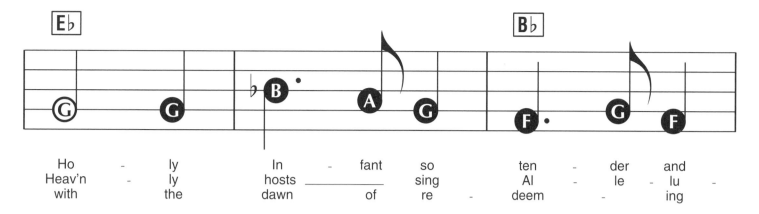

Ho	-	ly		In	-	fant	so		ten	-	der	and
Heav'n	-	ly		hosts			sing		Al	-	le	-	lu	-
with		the		dawn		of	re	-	deem		-	ing

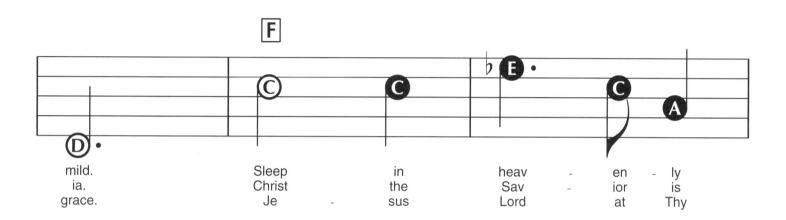

mild.		Sleep		in		heav	-	en	-	ly
ia.		Christ		the		Sav	-	ior	is
grace.		Je	-	sus		Lord		at		Thy

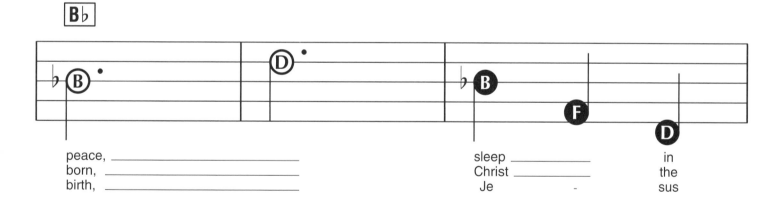

peace, _____		sleep _____		in
born, _____		Christ _____		the
birth, _____		Je	-	sus

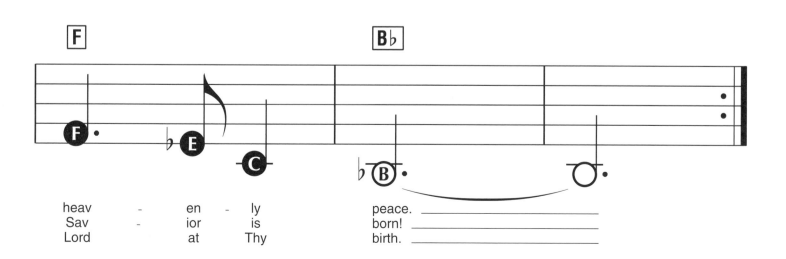

heav	-	en	-	ly		peace. _____
Sav	-	ior		is		born! _____
Lord		at		Thy		birth. _____

Up on the Housetop

Registration 5
Rhythm: Fox Trot or Swing

Words and Music by
B.R. Handy

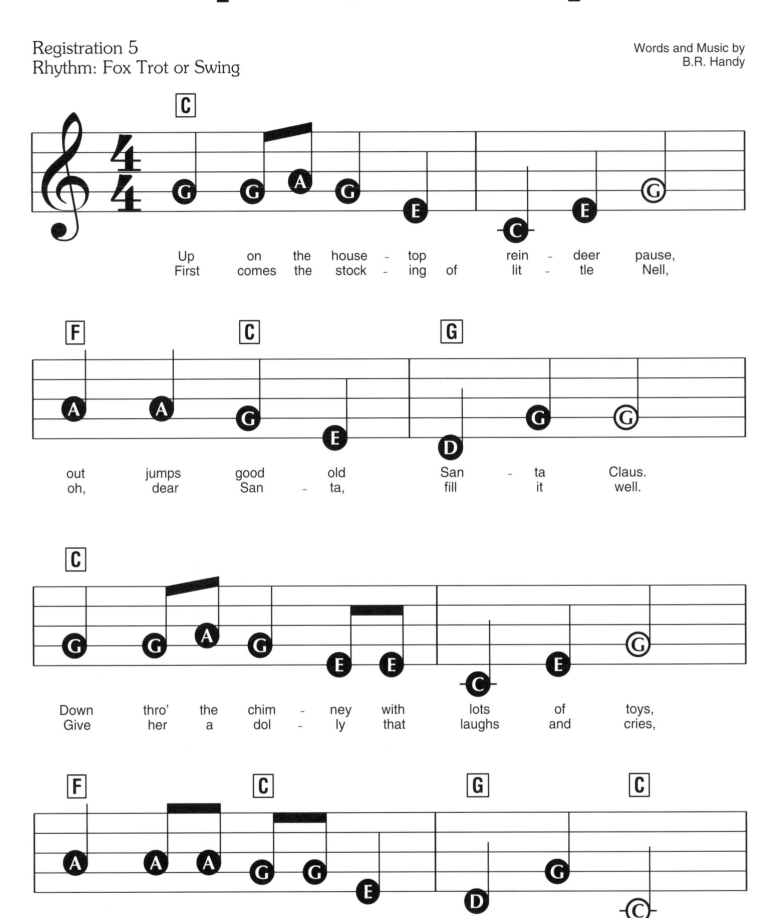

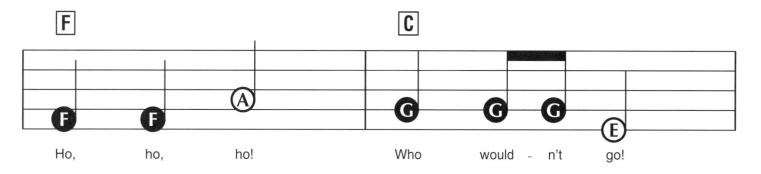

Ho, ho, ho! Who would-n't go!

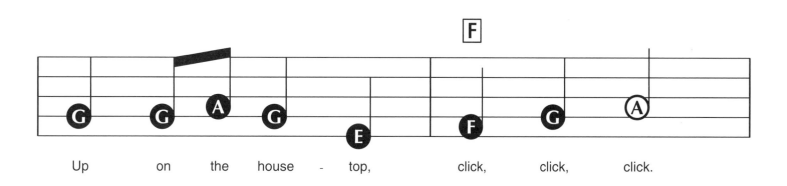

Ho, ho, ho! Who would-n't go! _____

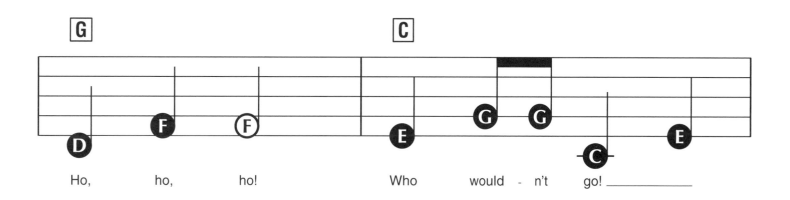

Up on the house-top, click, click, click.

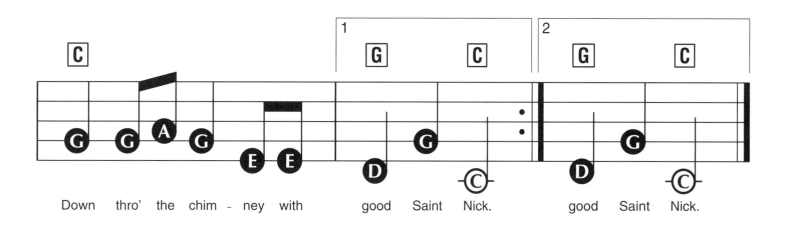

Down thro' the chim-ney with good Saint Nick. good Saint Nick.

Registration Guide

- Match the Registration number on the song to the corresponding numbered category below. Select and activate an instrumental sound available on your instrument.

- Choose an automatic rhythm appropriate to the mood and style of the song. (Consult your Owner's Guide for proper operation of automatic rhythm features.)

- Adjust the tempo and volume controls to comfortable settings.

Registration

1	Mellow	Flutes, Clarinet, Oboe, Flugel Horn, Trombone, French Horn, Organ Flutes
2	Ensemble	Brass Section, Sax Section, Wind Ensemble, Full Organ, Theater Organ
3	Strings	Violin, Viola, Cello, Fiddle, String Ensemble, Pizzicato, Organ Strings
4	Guitars	Acoustic/Electric Guitars, Banjo, Mandolin, Dulcimer, Ukulele, Hawaiian Guitar
5	Mallets	Vibraphone, Marimba, Xylophone, Steel Drums, Bells, Celesta, Chimes
6	Liturgical	Pipe Organ, Hand Bells, Vocal Ensemble, Choir, Organ Flutes
7	Bright	Saxophones, Trumpet, Mute Trumpet, Synth Leads, Jazz/Gospel Organs
8	Piano	Piano, Electric Piano, Honky Tonk Piano, Harpsichord, Clavi
9	Novelty	Melodic Percussion, Wah Trumpet, Synth, Whistle, Kazoo, Perc. Organ
10	Bellows	Accordion, French Accordion, Mussette, Harmonica, Pump Organ, Bagpipes